CONTEMPORARY'S
Reading and Critical Thinking
In the Content Areas

Martha J. Barnes

Senior Editor
Mark Boone

CB
CONTEMPORARY
BOOKS
CHICAGO · NEW YORK

The author extends a special thank you to Dr. Gloria J.
Taylor and Virginia Jackson-Staples for their careful review
of the manuscript and to students and colleagues for their
valuable contributions to the writing of this book.

Published by Contemporary Books, Inc.
180 North Michigan Avenue, Chicago, Illinois 60601
Manufactured in the United States of America
International Standard Book Number: 0-8092-4478-0

Published simultaneously in Canada by
Fitzhenry & Whiteside
91 Granton Drive
Richmond Hill, Ontario L4B 2N5
Canada

Editorial Director
Caren Van Slyke

Editorial
Karen Schenkenfelder
Julie Landau
Lori Lewis-Chapman
Lisa Dillman
Deborah Donberg
Kathy Osmus

Editorial/Production Manager
Patricia Reid

Cover Design
Lois Koehler

Photo Researcher
Julie Laffin

Art & Production
Sue Springston
Rosemary Morrissey-Herzberg

Typography
Carol Schoder

Cover photos © Image Bank

Contents

Acknowledgments

We gratefully acknowledge those who have granted permission to reprint the following:

Photo on page 1 by Spencer Grant/ MGA Chicago.

Photo on page 2 by the Bettmann Archive.

Poem on page 7, "Poor Girl," from *Oh Pray My Wings Are Gonna Fit Me Well* by Maya Angelou, copyright © 1975 by Maya Angelou. Reprinted by permission of Random House, Inc.

Photo on page 9 by A P/Wide World Photos.

Poem on page 10, "Résumé," from *The Portable Dorothy Parker.* Copyright 1926, renewed © 1954 by Dorothy Parker. Reprinted by permission of Viking Penguin Inc.

Cartoon on page 11 from "Dunigan's People." Reprinted with special permission of NAS, Inc.

Cartoon on page 15 by Dick Locher. Reprinted by permission: Tribune Media Services.

Excerpt on page 21 reprinted with permission of Macmillan Publishing Company from *Manchild in the Promised Land* by Claude Brown. Copyright © 1965 by Claude Brown.

Excerpt on pages 25–26 from *One Flew over the Cuckoo's Nest* by Ken Kesey, copyright © 1962. Reprinted by permission of Viking Penguin Inc.

Photo on page 26 © Shooting Star.

Photo on page 34 © Jennifer Bishop/ Stock Boston.

Photo on page 42 © Bob Daemmrich/ Stock Boston.

Photo on page 46 by Mark Peters/ Black Star.

Essay on page 56, "A Writer Needs An Ear for Words," from *The Best of Sydney J. Harris* by Sydney J. Harris. Copyright © 1975 by Sydney J. Harris. Reprinted by permission of Houghton Mifflin Company.

Selection on pages 60–62, an abridgment of *The War Prayer* by Mark Twain. Copyright © 1923, 1951 by the Mark Twain Company. Reprinted by permission of Harper & Row, Publishers, Inc.

Photo on page 65 by Robert Frerck/ Odyssey Productions.

Photo on page 67 © Eric Neurath/ Stock Boston.

Excerpt on page 70 from *Twelve Angry Men* © 1956 by Reginald Rose. Reprinted by permission of International Creative Management, Inc.

Short story on pages 74–76, "The Gentleman from Rio En Medio," by Juan A.A. Sedillo from *We are All Chicanos*, edited by Philip D. Ortega.

Anecdote on page 81 © Paulette Pennington-Jones.

Photo on page 83 by Frank Siteman/ MGA Chicago.

Photo on page 84 © Jerry Howard/ Stock Boston.

Short story on pages 90–93, "After You, My Dear Alphonse," from *The Lottery and Other Stories* by Shirley Jackson. Copyright 1948, 1949 by Shirley Jackson. Copyright renewed © 1976, 1977 by Laurence Hyman, Barry Hyman, Mrs. Sarah Webster, and Mrs. Joanne Schnurer. Originally appeared in *The New Yorker.* Reprinted by permission of Farrar, Straus and Giroux, Inc.

Photo on page 90 © Anestis Diakopoulous/Stock Boston.

Passage on page 97, "Impeaching a President," from *Writing With a Purpose* by James M. McCrimman, copyright © Houghton Mifflin Company.

Photo on page 102 from UPI/ Bettmann Newsphotos.

The editor has made every effort to trace the ownership of all copyrighted material, and necessary permissions have been secured in most cases. Should there prove to be a question regarding the use of any material, regret is hereby expressed for such error. Upon notification of any such oversight, proper acknowledgment will be made in future editions.

To the Instructor

Reading and Critical Thinking in the Content Areas is designed to help students develop the higher-level reading and thinking skills needed for success in school, in the workplace, and in their everyday lives.

This book is divided into two sections—**critical reading** and **critical thinking**. Critical reading involves the skills that help students understand what a writer is saying. Critical thinking involves the skills that help them judge the worth and believability of what the writer says and analyze *how* the writer is saying it.

Reading and Critical Thinking in the Content Areas exposes students to a variety of materials: poems, stories, editorial cartoons, articles, and editorials. The inclusion of readings and visuals from the content areas of literature, health science, and social studies helps students see how to adapt reading strategies to the special demands of different kinds of subject matter. Thus, students will better understand what they read and will appreciate the technique that goes into a piece of writing.

This book is designed to be used independently by students, but in the opinion of experts, critical-thinking skills are most effectively taught under a teacher's guidance. Therefore, it is highly recommended that you work through the material with your students, perhaps an exercise at a time.

Some of the thinking skills included in this book are applied to controversial issues. Faulty reasoning, invalid conclusions, author's bias, persuasive techniques, and other strategies are sometimes treated in the context of issues that are likely to generate spirited debate. This instructional approach is intended to help students see firsthand the dangers of unsound reasoning and thinking. For exercises such as these, a teacher's guidance is particularly important in helping students to examine and evaluate the logic of material they read or messages they hear in the media.

Many of the reading and thinking skills fall within the hierarchy of Bloom's taxonomy and may be classified under the cognitive levels of comprehension/interpretation, application, analysis, and evaluation. "Think and Write" activities, appearing throughout, fall under the synthesis category of Bloom's taxonomy. The list on page vi correlates the 16 skills to these levels.

Cognitive Level	Skill
comprehension/ application	stated main idea
	unstated main idea
	inferences
	conclusions from facts
	sequence
	predictions and outcomes
	cause and effect
	comparison/contrast
	connotation/denotation
analysis	fact, opinion, hypothesis
	invalid conclusions
	analogy
	persuasive techniques
evaluation	stereotypes
	values
	author's bias

Other features in this book are notable:

- two cumulative review activities enabling students to review skills covered
- a detailed answer key that provides explanations for the correct answers

The skills in this book move from the simple to the complex, and the difficulty of the readings and visuals varies accordingly. Students, faced with reading passages that range in difficulty, will be motivated by the high-interest content of the material. Research has shown that if students are interested in the subject matter, they can tackle more difficult vocabulary and complex sentence structure than they ordinarily work with. Thus, students who complete this text will become more competent and confident readers.

This book can be used as a springboard for further activity in critical thinking. By using some of the instructional approaches included in it, you can adapt material that you find in papers, magazines, and other formats for your own use in teaching critical thinking in the classroom.

To the Student

Welcome to Contemporary's *Reading and Critical Thinking in the Content Areas.* In this book, you will be learning skills that will help you become a more careful reader and thinker in your everyday life.

This book includes poems, articles, short stories, editorial cartoons, and editorials that are related to topics in literature, health science, and social studies.

This book has two sections—*critical reading* and *critical thinking.* Critical reading involves the skills that help you understand what a writer is saying. Critical thinking involves the skills that help you to judge the worth and believability of what the writer says and analyze *how* the writer is saying it. The book begins with shorter selections and moves to longer ones as your reading skills get stronger.

This book uses symbols that tell you that an exercise is beginning and the subject area it covers. These symbols are:

social studies    science    literature

Throughout this book, there are a number of features designed to help you learn. These include:

- photographs that highlight many of the readings

- "Think and Write" activities that give you a chance to practice thinking and writing skills

- special tips that help you apply a skill to a new situation

- two skill review exercises that give you a chance to test your progress in the reading and thinking skills

- an answer key that explains the correct answers for the exercises

As you do the exercises in this book, keep in mind that critical reading and thinking can become a part of your life. A good way to sharpen these skills is to apply critical reading and thinking skills to material you read in newspapers and magazines and to the messages you see on television and hear on the radio.

1 Critical-Reading Skills

When you read critically, you read to understand the writer's message and the steps he or she followed to get the message across. Just what makes up a writer's message? It is composed of *words* put together in a certain *pattern* to form ideas. The words and patterns used depend on the writer's purpose for writing.

In this section, you will practice reading different forms of writing. You will identify main ideas and practice finding the main idea when it is not stated. Also, you will put together facts to draw conclusions, make predictions, and identify organizing patterns. Finally, you will look carefully at words, the "tools of the trade" for writers. By studying the meaning of words, you will be able to see why writers choose the words they do.

1 What Is the Message?

Reading and writing cannot be separated. Writers write to be read. A writer has a purpose. The purpose may be to inform, to persuade, or to entertain. When creating a message, a writer must always keep the reader in mind. When reading, the reader must always think about the writer's intention.

When reading, a reader must bring the necessary background to what he or she reads. Background includes life experience, stored knowledge, and common language. By putting background with the message, the reader is able to understand what the writer is saying.

Readers' backgrounds are different. What one person may get from a message (and bring to it) will differ from what another gets. It is the writer's job, however, to make it as easy as possible for the reader to understand the message.

Writers have different ways to get their ideas across. Sometimes their message is loud and clear. The message tells the reader at the beginning what he or she will read about. At other times, the message may be understated, if stated at all. Then the reader must put forth more effort to understand what the writer means. This is mainly true for stories and poems.

In this chapter, you will practice your skills in interpreting a writer's message by

- summarizing the main idea
- making inferences
- drawing conclusions
- predicting outcomes

When you read, ask yourself often: What is the writer saying? What does the writer mean?

The Stated Main Idea

Summarizing the *main idea* is a skill that you perform daily without even thinking about it. For instance, if you gave someone the results of a championship football game, you wouldn't deliver a play-by-play account of what actually happened on the field. You would, instead, give a short version of the events that include only the main idea *(who won?)* and the important details *(by what score? by whose efforts?)*

In materials that you read, the following questioning strategy can help you find the main idea and the important details that support it. You should ask yourself the five fact questions:

- WHO does the event involve?
- WHEN did it take place?
- WHAT event took place?
- WHERE did it take place?
- HOW did it happen?

Let's see how this method can be applied to a reading passage. Read the passage below. As you read, ask yourself the five questions.

The Case of the Disappearing Checks

In the late 1980s, banking fraud reached new heights. The practice of check-kiting—writing bad checks—was outdone by the passing of disappearing checks.

The scam involved cheating banks in the Midwest, South, and West out of thousands of dollars. First, the crooks opened phony accounts. Then they cashed chemically treated checks against the accounts. Only hours after being presented to tellers for cash, the checks turned to confetti! In Chicago alone, checks totaling $50,000 were cashed. According to the FBI, once the checks had been cashed, the crooks closed the accounts.

Bank tellers were advised to take several measures to prevent being cheated. One step was to photocopy any check that had an oily surface. By taking such an action, the FBI hoped to catch the culprits and solve the case of the disappearing checks.

To identify the main idea of this passage, apply the five-question method in the following way:

WHO?	crooks
WHAT?	cheated banks out of thousands of dollars
WHERE?	in the Midwest, South, and West
WHEN?	the late 1980s
HOW?	by cashing chemically treated checks that turned into confetti hours after they were cashed

Main idea sentence: In the late 1980s, crooks cheated banks in the Midwest, South, and West out of thousands of dollars by cashing chemically treated checks that turned into confetti hours after they were cashed.

TIP: Often, titles and headlines contain key ideas that point to the main idea. Sometimes you can predict what the main idea will be by reading the titles.

Read the following passage. Then answer the questions and fill in the chart below. Use the facts from the chart to write a main idea sentence.

Rosa Parks Sparks Boycott

On December 1, 1955, in Montgomery, Alabama, a petite black woman was on her way home from work. She boarded a bus and sat in the "colored section." As more and more people got on, a white man was left standing. When the driver asked three black people to stand so that the white man could sit down, they did. But when the driver asked Rosa Parks to, she refused to give up her seat. She told him that she was not moving because she was tired and had paid her fare like everybody else. The driver threatened to have her arrested. When she still refused to move, he called the police.

The Parks case sparked the Montgomery bus boycott led by Dr. Martin Luther King, Jr. The boycott, which lasted a year, was the beginning of a movement that made segregation of public places in the South illegal.

WHO?	
WHAT?	
WHERE?	
WHEN?	
HOW?	

Main idea sentence: _____

_____

_____

THINK & WRITE: Henry David Thoreau served a jail sentence rather than pay a tax that was levied to support the Mexican-American War. He, like Rosa Parks, believed that citizens have the right to disobey laws that they think are unjust. Do you agree or disagree with Thoreau's and Parks's positions?

Answers and explanations start on page 110.

Read the passage below, and circle the correct answer for each question that follows.

Tired Hearts

The average human heart beats about 100,000 times a day and pumps about 2,000 gallons of blood a day. But even the heart gets tired and sometimes needs a rest. This fact was proved by medical researchers from the University of Pennsylvania.

In a study, twenty-one strong and healthy athletes took part in the "Ironman" triathlon held in Hawaii. The triathlon consisted of three events. The first was a 2.4-mile swim, the second a 26-mile run, and the third a 112-mile bicycle race.

The researchers learned that, after the triathlon, the athletes' hearts did not contract as well with each beat. Nor did their hearts pump as much blood between beats. However, twenty-four hours later, the athletes' hearts were again beating about 100,000 times daily and pumping almost 2,000 gallons of blood.

1. The main idea of the passage is that

   a. athletes do not suffer from heart fatigue
   b. a triathlon includes fewer events than a decathlon
   c. running 26 miles is less stressful than biking 112 miles
   d. exercise does not cause permanent damage to athletes
   e. an overworked heart does not work at peak levels

2. Which of the following statements does *not* help you to identify the main idea?

   a. The University of Pennsylvania has reliable sports researchers.
   b. After athletes participated in a triathlon, their hearts did not pump the normal amount of blood.
   c. Athletes who participated in the "Ironman" triathlon swam 2.4 miles, ran 26 miles, and biked 112 miles.
   d. The hearts of athletes get tired.
   e. Twenty-four hours after the athletes participated in the triathlon, their hearts worked normally.

Answers and explanations start on page 110.

Read the poem "Poor Girl" and answer the questions that follow.

Poor Girl

You've got another love
　　and I know it
Someone who adores you
　　just like me
Hanging on your words
　　like they were gold
Thinking that she understands
　　your soul
Poor Girl
　　　Just like me.

You're breaking another heart
　　and I know it
And there's nothing
　　I can do
If I try to tell her
　　what I know
She'll misunderstand
　　and make me go
Poor Girl
　　Just like me.

You're going to leave her too
　　and I know it
She'll never know
　　what made you go
She'll cry and wonder
　　what went wrong
Then she'll begin
　　to sing this song
Poor Girl
　　Just like me.

—by Maya Angelou

1. The speaker is the person who tells the poem. The main point
expressed by the poem is that the

  a. speaker is jealous of the girl her ex-boyfriend is dating
  b. speaker's new boyfriend knows what she feels
  c. speaker wants to give advice to her ex-boyfriend's new girlfriend
  d. speaker's new boyfriend has a history of breaking girls' hearts

2. The title "Poor Girl" is a clue to the main idea because the words *poor girl* suggest

    a. poverty
    b. pity
    c. fear
    d. innocence

Answers and explanations start on page 110.

The Unstated Main Idea

You have practiced summarizing the main idea by using the five-question method. Sometimes, however, the main point of an article is not stated. Instead, the author provides details or key ideas that point to the main idea. The reader must put all the facts together and determine the main idea. This is called **inferring the main idea**.

Read the paragraph below to discover the main idea.

To Smoke or Not to Smoke?

In San Francisco, as in many other U.S. cities, smoking is not permitted in public buildings and in many offices. In addition, many restaurants across the nation have established nonsmoking sections for customers who are offended by tobacco smoke.

The federal government has even required that smoking be banned on flights whose travel time is less than two hours. One airline, Northwest, has taken an even more extreme position. It bans smoking on *all* flights except those going to Europe, Asia, and Hawaii.

From the details provided, choose the unstated main idea from the statements listed below.

a. The link between smoking and lung cancer, heart disease, and emphysema has been proved.
b. Smokers are being deprived of their constitutional rights.
c. Nonsmokers outnumber smokers in America.
d. Nonsmokers are winning the battle against secondhand smoke in public places.

If you chose *d*, you chose the correct answer. The entire thrust of the paragraph is the impact nonsmokers are having in public places. The places discussed are:

- public buildings and offices
- restaurants
- airplanes

Although it is not stated directly, the entire paragraph shows nonsmokers winning the battle against secondhand smoke in public places.

> **TIP:** To find the unstated main idea, list the key ideas or details. Usually, they "add up" or point to a central thought that the paragraph is getting across.

Read the poem, then answer the questions that follow.

Résumé

Razors pain you;
Rivers are damp;
Acids stain you;
And drugs cause cramp;
Guns aren't lawful;
Nooses give;
Gas smells awful;
You might as well live.

—by Dorothy Parker

1. This poem is mainly about

    a. murder
    b. death
    c. suicide
    d. life

2. Which statement *best* summarizes the poet's feelings?

    a. There are many different ways of killing yourself.
    b. Death is the last stage of existence.
    c. Suicide is more trouble than it's worth.
    d. There is no easy way to die.
    e. Life is too beautiful and precious to waste.

3. "Résumé" is a clever title for this poem. Which of the following definitions is *not* related to the main idea of the poem?

    a. A résumé is a short account of a person's qualifications for seeking a job.
    b. Resume can mean "to begin again" or "to recover."
    c. A résumé is another name for a summary; the poem summarizes ways to end life.

4. This poem is effective *mainly* because the poet

    a. treats a serious subject with humor
    b. uses rhyming words
    c. lists seven ways of taking one's life

THINK & WRITE: Do you think people have a right to kill themselves? What might motivate a person to take his or her life?

Answers and explanations start on page 110.

Sometimes a cartoonist expresses a point humorously. Study the cartoon below to find the hidden main idea.

Reprinted with permission of NAS, Inc. © 1988, North American Syndicate, Inc.

1. What best summarizes the cartoonist's message?

   a. Thieves are everywhere.
   b. The Internal Revenue Service (IRS) office is a hangout for robbers.
   c. The Internal Revenue Service robs the American taxpayer.
   d. Taxpayers leaving the IRS should beware of robbers.

2. In the spaces below, put a check before the details that "add up" to the main idea.

   ☐ **a.** A taxpayer has just settled with the IRS.

   ☐ **b.** The taxpayer has money in his briefcase.

   ☐ **c.** The taxpayer is being arrested for holding up the IRS.

   ☐ **d.** The taxpayer is not afraid of the robber.

   ☐ **e.** The gunman wants to kill the taxpayer.

   ☐ **f.** The taxpayer did not receive a refund from the IRS.

   ☐ **g.** The gunman is "sticking up" the taxpayer.

Answers and explanations start on page 110.

Read the untitled passage below, then answer the questions that follow.

Have you ever wondered how one person can take drink after drink and not get drunk, while another is intoxicated after having only one?

According to the National Institute on Alcohol Abuse and Alcoholism, the effect of alcohol does not depend on how many drinks a person has. It depends on how fast alcohol is absorbed into the bloodstream and how quickly it is eliminated from the body. The more quickly alcohol is absorbed into the bloodstream, the sooner the drinker feels its effects. Also, the more quickly it is eliminated from the body, the less likely the drinker is to get drunk.

One factor that affects how alcohol is absorbed is the amount of water the drinker's body contains. Another factor is the percentage of body fat a person has. Fat cells contain very little water. Generally, women have a higher percentage of body fat than men do. Therefore, women absorb more alcohol through the bloodstream than do men.

1. The best title for this passage would be

   a. How to Hold Your Liquor
   b. Why Men Can Consume More Alcohol than Women
   c. How to Avoid Alcoholism
   d. The Effect of Alcohol on the Body

2. Place a check before the statements that the details in the passage support.

   ☐ **a.** Thin men are likely to get drunk more quickly than fat men.

   ☐ **b.** Women do not get drunk as quickly as men.

   ☐ **c.** Drinking plenty of water can slow the rate at which alcohol is absorbed.

   ☐ **d.** Carbonated mixers speed the rate at which alcohol is absorbed.

   ☐ **e.** If a man and woman of equal weight take the same number of drinks, the woman will get drunk more quickly.

3. The information in the passage might be used to explain why

    a. alcohol abuse is on the rise
    b. people prefer mixed drinks
    c. some men try to take advantage of women who drink
    d. the sale of alcohol was banned during the 1920s

4. List five things from the passage that can determine how quickly a person may get drunk.

    a. _____

    b. _____

    c. _____

    d. _____

    e. _____

Answers and explanations start on page 111.

Inferences

When you infer, you "read between the lines" to figure out what is being said. For example, if you called a friend and she responded by saying, "Oh, it's you," you might infer from the comment and tone that she was expecting to hear from someone else or that she didn't want to talk to you. You had to take a hint from the response and tone.

Much like a detective who solves a mystery, you can make inferences from what a writer has suggested. To infer the writer's message, follow these steps:

- Gather clues and details (evidence).
- Analyze (think carefully about) the evidence.
- Make a decision based on these facts.
- Test your decision against the facts given.

Let's apply this method to the following paragraph. Pay close attention to the evidence that helps you make an inference.

> You are stuck in traffic on an expressway at noontime. Usually few cars are traveling the expressway at that time of day. All of a sudden, you hear sirens and see flashing lights. Then an ambulance and police cars speed by. As you inch closer to the flashing lights ahead of you, you observe two overturned cars. What might you infer from what you have seen and heard?

You might guess that someone has been injured in an automobile accident. Let's examine the evidence that led you to this conclusion.

Gather Evidence
- A traffic jam during non-rush hours
- Sirens and flashing lights
- Speeding ambulance and police cars
- Overturned cars

Analyze Evidence
- Traffic jams seldom occur during midday.
- Flashing lights usually mean an emergency.
- A speeding ambulance means someone is hurt.

Evaluate Your Conclusion
- Based on what you observed, heard, and already know about traffic jams, emergency vehicles, and car accidents, you could infer that someone has been injured in an autombile accident.

TIP: In making inferences, put *all* the clues, facts, or details together. If facts are incomplete, you cannot make a valid inference. That would be jumping to conclusions.

Study the cartoon below and answer the following questions.

1. Based on the information in the cartoon, you could infer that

    a. people without experience can't get entry-level jobs

    b. a double standard exists for ordinary citizens looking for a job and politicians running for president

    c. a president doesn't need experience because he has to hire other people to assist him in his work

    d. if no one had taken a chance on the president when he was hired for his first job, he might never have become president

2. From this cartoon, you could infer that the cartoonist would be most critical of which of the following presidential candidates of 1988?

    a. George Bush, the vice president of the United States

    b. Pat Robertson, a religious leader

    c. Albert Gore, a U.S. senator from Tennessee

    d. Michael Dukakis, governor of Massachusetts

Answers and explanations start on page 111.

Read the passage below and answer the questions that follow.

Left and Right Brain Power

The human brain is often described as having two halves—a left hemisphere and a right hemisphere. Each half performs a certain function. The left half controls the ability to see detailed patterns, while the right half controls the ability to see the whole picture. People who are left-brain "dominant" tend to be better at performing detail-oriented work. Right-brain "dominant" people generally are better at performing tasks that require seeing the "big picture."

Research has shown that people respond to what they see differently, depending on which half of the brain dominates. For example, in distinguishing faces, the left half of the brain focuses on special features such as the presence of glasses, the thickness of lips, and the shape of the nose. On the other hand, the right half of the brain usually sees the face in its entirety.

Although people are stronger in using one-half of the brain, we need to use both halves. The challenge for people, be they left-brain or right-brain dominant, is to work on improving the part of the brain that is less developed.

1. The passage implies that left-brain dominant people

   a. are no different than right-brain dominant people
   b. are less talented than right-brain dominant people
   c. are mistreated by the larger society
   d. approach problems differently than right-brain dominant people

2. List three examples of evidence for the inference you chose.

   a. _____

   b. _____

   c. _____

3. There's an expression that says "A person can't see the forest for the trees." According to the passage, left-brained people would see the _____, while right-brained people would see the _____.

4. The expression might be seen as a putdown of which type of person?

   _____

THINK & WRITE: Based on the information in the passage, are you primarily a right-brained or left-brained person? Why?

Answers and explanations start on page 111.

Read the following summary of "The Monkey's Paw" by W. W. Jacobs, and answer the questions that follow.

Mr. and Mrs. White and their son Herbert gathered around the fireplace to hear Sergeant-Major Morris tell a story about a monkey's paw. The paw had been placed under a spell and had the power to grant three wishes for three different men. Sergeant-Major Morris, himself, received the paw after the first owner's final wish—death—had been granted.

The paw had caused great suffering for Sergeant-Major Morris. To be rid of it, he tried to destroy it by throwing the paw into the fire. Ignoring the Sergeant-Major's warning about the paw's dangers, however, Mr. White retrieved it.

Doubting the paw's powers, Mr. White asked how a person was to make the wishes. The Whites didn't believe that the paw could do them harm. Morris told them how to make the wishes.

Mr. White's first wish was for 200 pounds to pay off his mortgage, but when the mail came to his home the next day, Mrs. White found only bills. The second day, however, a visitor from Herbert's job came to express the company's sympathy: Herbert had been caught in machinery at work and was killed. The visitor delivered insurance money in the amount of 200 pounds.

A week after Herbert's funeral, a grief-stricken Mrs. White forced her husband to make a second wish. Hours later, they heard a knock at the door. The knocking got louder and louder. As Mrs. White struggled to open the bolted door, Mr. White searched desperately for the paw to make his third wish. Mrs. White freed the bolt just as he found the paw to make the final wish. As he made it, the knocking stopped suddenly, and the door opened. A cold wind rushed up the staircase.

1. A good title for this story might be

a. Magical Powers Can't Change Your Life
b. You Get What You Deserve
c. Be Careful About What You Ask for—You Just Might Get It
d. Death Comes in Many Disguises

2. Which of the following ideas is *not* suggested in the story?

a. Grief sometimes makes people do unreasonable things.
b. The monkey's paw is a wicked and horrible symbol.
c. People sometimes put their faith in charms.
d. Mrs. White cares more about the insurance money than she does about her son's death.

3. Does this story take place in the United States? _____

What one clue word helped you decide? _____

_____

4. What is Mr. White's second wish? _____

What clue helped you to decide? _____

_____

5. What is Mr. White's third wish? _____

What clue helped you to decide? _____

_____

THINK & WRITE: Why would the first owner of the paw have asked for death as his final wish? What does this suggest about his first two wishes?

Answers and explanations start on page 111.

Conclusions from Facts

To draw a *conclusion*, you must first consider all of the facts provided in a given situation. For example, suppose you invite a co-worker to lunch and she refuses because she says she brought her own lunch. Later, however, you see her eating lunch with another co-worker. When you ask her to go to the office party with you, she replies that she isn't going. Then, she shows up with the same co-worker with whom she had lunch, and she gives you no explanation.

From these facts, which one of the following conclusions can you come to?

_____ **a.** She is a loner.

_____ **b.** She doesn't care to socialize with co-workers.

_____ **c.** She prefers to keep her relationship with you on a professional level.

If you chose *c*, you chose the best conclusion, since on two occasions she refused to socialize with you and went with another co-worker. Choice *a* is not the best conclusion because no facts are provided to support the conclusion that she is a loner. Choice *b* is not the best conclusion because you saw her twice in the company of another co-worker. The facts "add up" to the conclusion in *c*.

> **T**IP: To draw a correct conclusion, list *all* of the facts available to you. Then think of reasonable explanations for the facts. Finally, eliminate any possible explanations that all the facts together do not support.

Study the pie graphs below. Then draw the conclusions that follow from the information provided.

Offenders and Victims

Recent crime statistics show that about one out of seven people in America has been the victim of a crime. These pie graphs provide information about two types of violent crimes and the relationships of the victim to the offender.

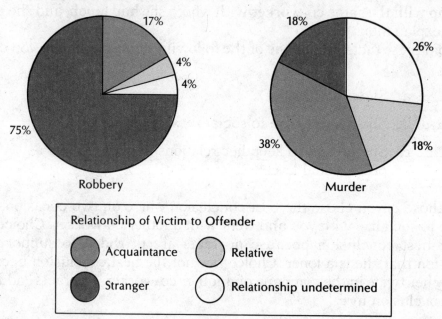

Adapted from graphs that appeared in the December 4, 1987, issue of *Scholastic Update*.

1. Answer the following questions based on the information included in the graphs.

   a. What percentage of people are killed by strangers? _____

   b. What percentage of homicide victims know the people who kill them? _____

   c. What percentage of people are killed by relatives? _____

   d. What percentage of victims know the people that rob them?

   _____

2. Write *yes* before each statement that represents a conclusion that can be drawn from the facts provided in the graphs. Write *no* before each statement that cannot be based on the facts given.

   _____ **a.** Most robbery cases are not reported to the police.

   _____ **b.** Most victims of homicides know the people who kill them.

_____ **c.** The percentage of people killed by strangers is the same as the percentage of people killed by relatives.

_____ **d.** More robberies are committed than any other violent crime.

_____ **e.** Most people do not know the people who rob them.

_____ **f.** Robberies rather than murders are more likely to be committed by strangers.

Answers and explanations start on page 112.

In the following excerpt from _Manchild in the Promised Land,_ by Claude Brown, Claude advises his mother to complain to the housing commission about her cold apartment. As you read the excerpt, think about his mother's reaction to filing a complaint. Then complete the activity that follows.

This day that I'd come up to talk was right after a big snowstorm. It was pretty cold. Mama was complaining about how cold it was. "Mama, why don't you complain to the landlord about this?"

"I called the office of the renting agency twice, and they said he wasn't in. When I called the third time, I spoke to him but he said that it wasn't his problem, and I'd have to fix it up myself. I ain't got no money to be getting these windows relined."

"Mama, that's a whole lot of stuff. I know better than that. Why don't you go up to the housing commission and complain about it?"

"I ain't got no time to be goin' no place complaining about nothin'. I got all this housework to do, and all this cookin' . . . ."

We went over to 145th Street. We were going to take the crosstown out to Broadway, to the temporary housing commission office. We were waiting there. Because of the snowstorm, the buses weren't running well, so we waited there for a long time. Mama said, "Look, we'd better wait and go some other time."

I knew she wanted to get out of this, and I knew if I let her go and put it off to another time, it would never be done. I said, "Mama, we can take a cab."

"You got any money? I ain't got none either. So we better wait until another time."

She waited there on the corner, and I went over to the pawnshop and pawned my ring. When I came back, we took a cab to Broadway and 145th Street, to the temporary housing commission office. When I got there, I told one of the girls at the window that I wanted to write out a complaint against a tenement landlord. . . .

I thought about the way Mama would go down to the meat market sometimes, and the man would sell her some meat that was spoiled, some old neck bones or some pig tails. Things that weren't too good even when they weren't spoiled. And sometimes she would say, "Oh, those things aren't too bad." She was scared to take them back, scared to complain until somebody said, "That tastes bad."

The statements below are based on the passage. For each statement, write a detail from the passage that would support it.

1. The mother is willing to risk her health to avoid complaining.

   Support: _____

   _____

2. The son is unselfish.

   Support: _____

   _____

3. The story takes place during the winter.

   Support: _____

   _____

4. The story takes place in New York City.

   Support: _____

   _____

Answers and explanations start on page 112.

Read the following passage, and complete the exercise that follows.

Zits Can Give Teens Fits

Acne is a common skin problem for teenagers. Acne is caused by too much oil being produced by the skin's oil glands. This disorder is especially common during the teen years because the production of sex hormones increases. When the excess oil comes into contact with bacteria, the bacteria set up an infection in the skin.

Acne comes in different forms. A blackhead, for instance, is one type that occurs when dead skin cells and oil get trapped in the ducts and hair follicles. A blackhead is so named because of the dark pigment in the skin cells that clog the ducts.

Sometimes the clogged skin ducts break open. This allows the oil and bacteria to spread to the surrounding tissue. When this occurs, pimples develop or the skin reddens. If the problem goes untreated, the skin becomes even more inflamed, destroying the tissue and causing scarring.

Mild cases of acne can normally be treated by deep cleansing the skin and using over-the-counter medication. More serious acne problems should be treated by a dermatologist. This skin specialist usually prescribes medication to help fight the bacterial infection. As an extra measure, people who have acne are advised to avoid foods that contain high levels of acid or fat.

Write *yes* before each statement that represents a conclusion that can be drawn from the facts in the passage. Write *no* before each statement that is not based on the facts in the passage.

_____ 1. Acne goes through several stages before scarring occurs.

_____ 2. Acne is primarily caused by eating fatty and acidic foods.

_____ 3. Teenagers are more likely to have acne than are adults.

_____ 4. Dirty skin is the chief cause of acne.

_____ 5. Fatty acids increase the amount of oil in the body.

_____ 6. Acne can be blamed on a hormonal imbalance in the body.

Answers and explanations start on page 112.

Predictions and Outcomes

When you *predict an outcome*, you guess what will happen next based on the pattern of events that happened before. For instance, if on a bright, warm summer day, the air suddenly turns cool, clouds blow in, and the sky darkens, you predict that it will rain. Further, if you look up into the sky and spot a bolt of lightning, you predict that a thunderclap will follow within seconds. Both of these predictions are based on the events that preceded them.

Similarly, in reading, you can increase your understanding of what you read by improving your ability to anticipate, or predict, what is likely to happen.

The following strategy can help you to predict an outcome:

- List the events or actions in order.
- Think about how the events and actions might be connected.
- Relate these events and actions to past experience.
- Make a reasonable guess as to what will happen based on the evidence and your own experience.

Read the following case study. Then choose the correct prediction based on the facts given.

Fickle Fitzpatrick

Mr. Fitzpatrick amazes me with his "weight reduction" programs. Just last year, for example, when he was keynote speaker at the employee banquet, he *gained* twenty pounds instead of losing the thirty he promised he would.

The year before that, he joined a health club. He exercised every day and consumed fewer calories. At the end of three months, however, he began making excuses about why he couldn't get to the spa more often.

After the health club failure, he joined Weight Watchers but stopped going because he was the only man who attended. As far as the Scarsdale Diet he was supposed to follow, forget it. Fitz's latest idea is to join a neighborhood walking club to "walk off" the weight.

Mr. Fitzpatrick announced plans to undergo hypnosis to lose weight. Based on his past record, you can reasonably predict that he will

_____ **a.** lose the weight he desires

_____ **b.** fail to follow through with his plan

_____ **c.** gain more weight than ever before

If you chose *b*, you predicted the correct outcome based on Mr. Fitzpatrick's past behavior. List three facts that you based your prediction on.

1. _____

2. _____

3. _____

Your prediction was likely based on three of these facts:

1. Mr. Fitzpatrick *gained* twenty pounds instead of losing thirty.
2. He joined a health club but stopped attending regularly.
3. He joined Weight Watchers but stopped going because he was the only man in attendance.
4. He didn't follow through with the Scarsdale Diet.

Each of the four facts shows Mr. Fitzpatrick's inability to stick to a plan. Based on these past events, it is highly unlikely that Mr. Fitzpatrick will follow through on his plan to undergo hypnosis to lose weight.

> **T**IP: In making predictions based on what you read, be sure that you have enough facts to support the prediction. Remember, a prediction is only a reasonable guess.

In the following excerpt from *One Flew over the Cuckoo's Nest*, Nurse Ratched explains to the patients the mental hospital staff's reason for punishing them. As you read the excerpt, notice how Nurse Ratched justifies the punishment given to them.

"Boys, I've given a great deal of thought to what I am about to do. I've talked it over with the doctor and with the rest of the staff. And we all came to the same conclusion—that your behavior concerning house duties three weeks ago was unspeakable. We waited this long to say anything, hoping that you men would take it upon yourselves to apologize for the rebellious way you acted. But not one of you has shown the slightest sign of remorse.

"Please understand. We do not impose certain rules and restrictions on you without a great deal of thought about their therapeutic value. A good many of you are in here because you could not adjust to rules of society in the outside world. You refused to face up to them and you tried to avoid them. At some time—perhaps in your childhood—you may have been allowed to get away with breaking the rules of society. When you broke a rule, you knew it. You wanted to be dealt with. And you needed to be

dealt with, but the punishment did not come. That foolish leniency on the part of your parents may have been the germ that grew into your present illness. It is difficult to enforce discipline in these surroundings. You must be able to see that. What can we do? You can't be arrested. You can't be put on bread and water. You must see that the staff has a problem. What can we do?"

1. Based on what the speaker says, the staff will probably

   a. send the men to a work farm
   b. recommend that the men get psychiatric help
   c. ignore the neglectful behavior and give the men another chance
   d. punish the men by taking away one of their favorite privileges

2. The speaker suggests that the men's confinement is partly due to all of the following *except*

   a. their parents' failure to discipline them as children
   b. their inability to cope with rules in the outside world
   c. their lack of job skills in the outside world
   d. their need for psychological therapy

Answers and explanations start on page 112.

Read the passage below, and answer the questions that follow.

The Insurance Game

Did you know that the job of certain people is to predict how long people will live? This prediction is based on data involving disease, sex, nutrition, and other information about the American population.

People who calculate life expectancy rates are called **actuaries**. Life expectancy is the length of time a person is expected to live. Actuaries put this information into tables, which insurance companies use to determine premiums. An insurance premium is the amount of money a customer pays on an insurance contract. Insurance companies are able to make profits because they take in more money in premiums than they must pay out in death claims.

In general, the younger a person is, the lower the premium will be. This is because most young people will live for quite a while longer, so the insurance company will not have to pay many death claims for young people in any one year. The company is gambling that most young people will live through the year.

On the other hand, the older a person is, the higher the premium will be. The older people are, the more likely they are to die during the year. Therefore, the company will probably have to pay more claims on older people. The company is guessing that more old people will die during the year.

1. Based on the facts in the passage above, insurance might be compared to a

   a. roll of the dice
   b. lottery
   c. betting game

2. Life insurance premiums for women usually are lower than those for men. This fact suggests that:

   a. Women are healthier than men.
   b. The number of women in the population is greater than the number of men.
   c. Women generally live longer than men.

3. Which of the following would most likely affect the premium that a person pays for life insurance?

   a. race
   b. health
   c. place of residence

Study the table below and answer the questions that follow.

Life Expectancy

Age	Number of Years Left to Live	
(in 1980)	Male	Female
10	61.6	66.7
15	56.9	61.7
20	52.3	57.0
25	47.8	52.3
30	43.2	47.6
35	38.6	42.9
40	34.0	38.3
45	29.6	33.8
50	25.3	29.5
55	21.2	25.3
60	17.5	21.2
65	14.0	17.3

Based on the Insurance Commissioners 1980 Standard Ordinary Mortality Table.

4. Fill in each blank with the correct answer from the chart.

   a. To what age are men expected to live who were 15 years old in 1980? _____

   b. To what age are women expected to live who were 25 years old in 1980? _____

   c. Men who were 40 years old in 1980 are expected to live how many years less than women born in the same year? _____

   d. Women who were 50 years old in 1980 are expected to live how many years longer than men born the same year? _____

5. For each of the following statements, write *T* on the line if the statement is true based on the information in the table. Write *F* if it is false.

_____ **a.** The life expectancy of men is higher than the life expectancy of women.

_____ **b.** Women who were 65 years old in 1980 were expected to live at least three years longer than men of the same age.

_____ **c.** In 1980, young people's life expectancy was short.

_____ **d.** Men who were 30 years old in 1980 can expect that most of them will live only until they are 61 years old.

THINK & WRITE: In some areas of the country, the life expectancy for infants is no better than that for poor, undeveloped Third World countries in Asia, Africa, and Latin America. What are some of the reasons for this?

Answers and explanations start on page 112.

2 What Pattern Is Followed?

Writers have many ways to organize their thoughts. Just as a cabinet-maker or dressmaker follows a pattern to create a product, so too does the writer.

For writers, a pattern is the framework on which their ideas hang. The more quickly you are able to follow a pattern in what you read, the better you will understand the message. Sometimes your ability to see a pattern early in a piece of writing can help you to predict what the writer is going to say even before you read it all.

Some subject areas use one pattern more often than another. For example, history writers frequently use the pattern of cause and effect. This is because the study of history is a study of causes and effects. Sequence, or time order, is also used in history because the writer's job is to cover events of a particular time period.

In this chapter, you will practice your skills in understanding three patterns:

- cause and effect
- sequence
- comparison and contrast

As you read each selection, ask yourself: What pattern is the writer using? Why did the writer choose this pattern? Would another pattern have worked as well for this topic?

Cause and Effect

When we talk about **cause and effect**, we are telling *why* something happens. For example, if Shop Rite Foods is the only store in your neighborhood, and all of the residents shop there, the management will be less likely to offer special deals to attract shoppers. However, if Buy Low Foods opens and offers lower prices and better service, it is likely to draw shoppers from the other store. As a result, Shop Rite Foods might have to offer deals to attract shoppers.

The opening of a new store (the cause) leads to lower prices and better service from the older store (the effect).

Every time you use the word *because* in explaining why something happens, you are showing a cause-and-effect relationship. In the sentence below, see if you can identify a cause-and-effect relationship.

> Abraham Lincoln signed the Emancipation Proclamation because he wanted to save the Union.

What is the action that occurred? _____

_____

Why did it happen? _____

_____

If you wrote: *Abraham Lincoln signed the Emancipation Proclamation*, you identified the **effect**—the *what* in the sentence.

If you wrote: *because he wanted to save the Union*, you identified the **cause**—the *why* in the sentence.

Now, let's change the order of ideas of the sentence:

> Because he wanted to save the Union, Abraham Lincoln signed the Emancipation Proclamation.

Compare the order of the words in this sentence to the order of the words in the earlier sentence. The cause-and-effect relationship remains the same even when the order of ideas changes.

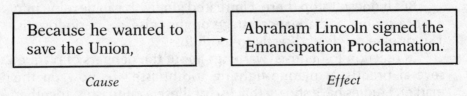

Because he wanted to save the Union,	→	Abraham Lincoln signed the Emancipation Proclamation.
Cause		*Effect*

Now try changing the order of the cause and effect. Rewrite the sentence below in the boxes provided.

Deaf students boycotted classes because they wanted a deaf person to be president of their school.

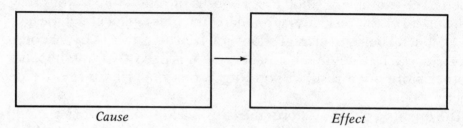

Cause   Effect

You should have rewritten the sentence this way:

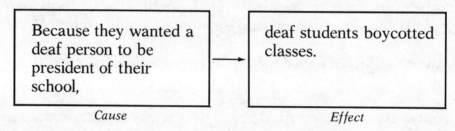

Because they wanted a deaf person to be president of their school,	→	deaf students boycotted classes.
Cause		Effect

TIP: These clue words usually show a cause-and-effect relationship: *because, since, as a result of, due to, therefore, consequently, follows, if ... then, brought about.*

Sometimes one cause can lead to more than one effect, and one effect can develop from many causes. The next passage provides an example of this. Read the passage, and complete the activity that follows.

Plaque Attack

If you eat on the run, without taking time to floss and brush your teeth, you are inviting an enemy called plaque into your mouth. Plaque is a sticky film of bacteria that gradually forms on your teeth. If plaque goes unchecked, the result can be a gum disease known as gingivitis. Signs of gingivitis include bleeding and red, swollen gums.

But it doesn't stop there. Untreated gingivitis can develop into a more serious and advanced stage of gum disease, periodontitis. This disease can lead directly to tooth loss.

In reaction to dentists' warnings about the dangers of plaque, several brands of plaque-fighting toothpaste are now on the market. Studies have shown that use of these toothpastes, together with frequent flossing and brushing, have reduced plaque considerably.

1. According to the passage, what three things cause plaque?

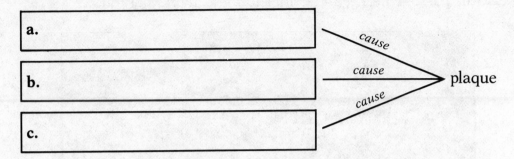

2. What is the first disease that plaque can lead to? _____

_____

3. What advanced stage of disease can untreated plaque lead to? _____

_____

4. What might be the final result of gum disease if it is not treated? ____

_____

5. What effect have dentists' warnings had on dental hygiene?

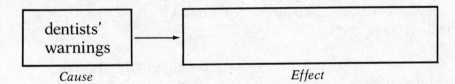

Answers and explanations start on page 113.

Read the passage below, and complete the activity that follows.

"Cop-outs for Dropouts: Who's to Blame?"

In some urban communities, almost half of the ninth-graders drop out before they complete high school. Who's to blame for this high dropout rate?

- Many parents feel that the rate is high because of the shrinking numbers of dedicated teachers. Also, they complain that the teaching of basic skills is inadequate.

- Teachers, on the other hand, feel that education begins at home. They blame parents for not reinforcing what their children are learning in the classroom. If children are not supervised properly, teachers say, they will spend much of their time watching television or hanging out.

- Parents aren't the only ones being blamed for the high dropout rates. Teachers fault the school system for spending too much money on administrative concerns rather than in the classroom. Teachers feel that fewer dollars should go toward administrative services and more toward hiring, training, and paying teachers. Such improvements will result in smaller classes. With smaller classes, there will be more time for individual or small-group instruction.

- Many officials of the school system point the finger at the teachers and the government. They believe that most teachers aren't giving their all. Moreover, school officials blame the government for not putting more dollars for education in its budget.

● When you ask the victims of the dropout rate—the students themselves—you get a startling answer. They blame *everybody* except themselves! According to students, the high dropout rate can be blamed on the lack of parental support, peer group pressure, overcrowded classrooms, lack of individual attention from teachers, and the lack of dedicated teachers and administrators. The government doesn't escape blame either. Students feel that support from both the government and private industry might help solve the problem.

1. In a sentence, write the *effect* that the passage discusses. _____

_____

Place a check before each cause that contributed to the effect you wrote above. You may check more than one.

2. According to parents, the causes are

☐ **a.** the students themselves

☐ **b.** gang activity

☐ **c.** drugs among students

☐ **d.** lack of dedicated teachers

☐ **e.** inadequate teaching of basic skills

3. According to the teachers, the causes are

☐ **a.** lack of support from parents

☐ **b.** the teachers themselves

☐ **c.** school administrators

☐ **d.** private industry

☐ **e.** peer group pressure

4. According to school administrators, the causes are

☐ **a.** too little government funding

☐ **b.** uncaring parents

☐ **c.** unprepared and undedicated teachers

☐ **d.** school administrators themselves

☐ **e.** private industry

5. According to the students, the causes are

- ☐ **a.** lack of discipline
- ☐ **b.** peer group pressure
- ☐ **c.** lack of parental support
- ☐ **d.** overcrowded classes
- ☐ **e.** a need to earn money by working

THINK & WRITE: "Copouts for Dropouts" suggests possible explanations for why many people drop out of school. Give one reason why you think there are so many dropouts. What do you think is a solution to this problem?

Answers and explanations start on page 113.

Read the passage below, and complete the activity that follows.

Against the Odds

"We want Terry!" the fans chanted. It was the last game of the season. Terry had looked forward to this moment for a long time. As far back as he could remember, he had wanted to be a superstar. As he looked around the college gym, Terry wondered how many scouts were there. For a moment, he could see himself leaving college at the end of his junior year to sign a million-dollar contract.

"I can always go back to college," he thought. "After all, with money, who needs a college degree?"

Terry could see his mother in her dream house. He even saw himself walking down the aisle with his childhood sweetheart.

Less than two minutes remained in the fourth quarter. The score was 96 to 94, with Terry's team trailing. The coach called "time out" and put Terry in the game.

Terry's teammates didn't waste any time getting the ball to him. By now, the fans were on their feet yelling, "Score, Terry, score!"

"I have to win this game," Terry thought. "My whole life depends on it."

As he made a move to the basket, Terry's ankle twisted, and he fell. Two rival players went down with him.

The clock stopped. Suddenly the crowd stood still. Terry's two opponents got up, but Terry couldn't move. The coach and the paramedics ran to the floor and tried to help Terry stand up. But the pain in his knee wouldn't let him.

Terry was rushed to the hospital where the x-rays showed he had a fractured kneecap. The outlook was that Terry needed extensive knee surgery and would have to postpone his professional basketball career indefinitely.

While the doctor was explaining the surgery and suggesting another career, Terry's mind was far away. He was thinking about his former teammates who had given in to life's bad breaks. Then his mind went to Dirk Jones, his idol, who had beaten the odds.

A doctor had told Dirk that he might never play ball again. But Dirk hadn't given up. With his coach's help, Dirk found a doctor who was able to perform the delicate surgery. The surgery was combined with a vigorous rehabilitation program. Together, they restored the strength and endurance of Dirk's knee. As a result, Dirk was back on the court within a year.

Terry's doctor continued to discourage Terry about a pro career. "Being a science teacher isn't a bad idea. . . . You've got the necessary health credits," he said.

"I'm gonna play pro ball, Doc," Terry said. "I may be down now, but I'm not down for the count!"

1. What do you think causes Terry's fall? _____

_____

2. What are the effects of Terry's fall? _____

_____

3. According to the passage, what could be the effect if a knee injury is treated promptly and a rehabilitation plan is followed?

   a. An athlete's knee will heal in three months.
   b. An athlete's disability will last for about a year.
   c. Sports medicine will be a popular field in which to specialize.
   d. Athletes will not need to wear knee braces.

4. The statement that Terry is "down but not down for the count" suggests that he

   a. is not giving up on his career goal
   b. will settle for becoming a science teacher
   c. is listening to the doctor's pep talk
   d. is thinking about his broken dreams

5. Why is "Against the Odds" an appropriate title for this story? _____

_____

Answers and explanations start on page 113.

Sequence

Writers often organize their ideas in the order in which they happen. The step-by-step ordering of events is called *time order* or *sequence*.

If you've ever followed a recipe to bake a cake, you had to follow a time-order pattern. The first step in making the batter is to cream together the shortening, eggs, and sugar before adding the flour. If you put the flour in and then add the other ingredients, chances are that the cake won't turn out the way it should.

Sequence is used especially in social studies when a writer covers historical events that happen over a period of time. Time order may also be used in science to list the steps in an experiment or to show the stages of a process. In literature, a writer of stories may center the action around a plot. A plot is a sequence of events.

The passage below explains how to make and use a salve to treat infections. The recipe for this home remedy comes from southern Appalachia. As you read this passage, look for words that signal time order. Underline the words that indicate the order of events or the passage of time.

A Salve That Can Save You Money

If you want to draw out the infection from a boil, sore, or cut, or treat a bruise, you may save some money by making your own salve.

Begin by making the main ingredient, tallow. Tallow is made by first taking the fat from beef. Then cook the fat in a little water, stirring it constantly so that it doesn't stick to the pan.

After all of the fat has been rendered (melted), strain the drippings, and set the tallow aside to harden. When the tallow has hardened, take a palmful and add a level teaspoon of brown sugar, a level teaspoon of salt, and a few drops of turpentine. Mix these ingredients well before adding the final one, a few drops of camphor oil.

The completed salve can now be applied directly to the wound and covered for about eight hours. If the infection is not cured in eight hours, repeat the application.

Were you able to find the words that signaled time order? You should have underlined the words *begin, first, then, after, when, before, final,* and *now*.

To test whether or not you understood the sequence of steps in making tallow, list them.

- Step 1: Take the fat from beef.
- Step 2: Cook fat in water, stirring constantly.
- Step 3: Strain the pan drippings.
- Step 4: Set the tallow aside to harden.
- Step 5: Mix the tallow, brown sugar, salt, and turpentine.
- Step 6: Add camphor oil.
- Step 7: Apply the salve.

TIP: These signals indicate a time-order pattern: first, second, third; next; before; later; last; earlier; final; then; after; since; finally; begin; *a* . . . *b* . . . *c* . . .; now; while; until.

Read the story below, and complete the activity that follows.

Senior Fights Back

Early one Tuesday morning just before daybreak, 66-year-old Sally Duncan was taking her usual morning walk in the park, when a lanky teenager suddenly appeared.

He threatened her with a knife and demanded the coin purse that hung from her neck. When he found only a key, he slapped her. Sally asked him, "What are you going to do next, kill me? I bet your mother would be proud," she said.

The boy then told her to shut up and glanced at her fifty-dollar running shoes. They were a birthday present from her grandchildren.

"Take the shoes off," he demanded. "Or I'll cut 'em off."

As Sally bent over, pretending to take off her shoes, she grabbed his wrist, forcing him to drop the knife. She kicked him in the groin. As he bent over, she belted him in the back with her elbow, and he fell to the ground.

From an apartment building nearby, a couple witnessed the entire scene and called the police, but not before they applauded Sally.

1. Arrange the following details in the order in which they occur in the story. Number the first event 1, the second 2, and so on.

    _____ **a.** A boy threatened Sally and demanded her purse.

    _____ **b.** Sally began her morning walk.

    _____ **c.** The boy found a key in Sally's purse.

    _____ **d.** Sally tried to make the boy feel ashamed.

    _____ **e.** Sally kicked and hit the boy to protect herself.

    _____ **f.** The boy threatened to cut Sally's shoes off.

    _____ **g.** The boy fell to the ground.

    _____ **h.** Witnesses applauded Sally and called the police.

2. The *best* underlying message from this incident is

    a. Crime Doesn't Pay
    b. Looks Are Deceiving
    c. Respect Your Elders
    d. Better Luck Next Time

3. From the facts in the story, you can infer that

    a. Sally's attacker wears the same size shoes as she does
    b. Sally is poor
    c. Sally has taken self-defense training
    d. Sally is stronger than the boy

4. Based on the events that occurred in the story, you can reasonably predict that

    a. the boy will never attack another elderly woman again
    b. the boy will be booked for attempted armed robbery
    c. Sally will never again take a walk in the park at daybreak
    d. Sally will refuse to press charges against the boy

Answers and explanations start on page 113.

In science, the steps in a process are often pictured in sequence. By following the steps shown in order, you can understand the beginning and end result of a process.

Study the illustration below, then complete the activity that follows.

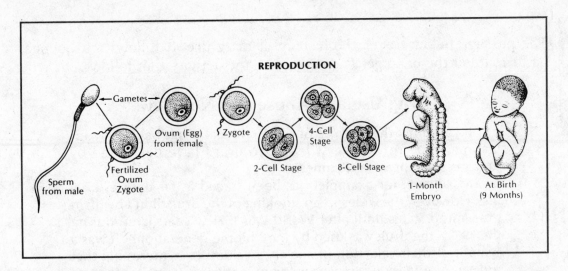

REPRODUCTION

Gametes

Sperm from male

Fertilized Ovum Zygote

Ovum (Egg) from female

Zygote

2-Cell Stage

4-Cell Stage

8-Cell Stage

1-Month Embryo

At Birth (9 Months)

Listed below are the steps in the human reproductive process. In the blanks provided, number the sentences and phrases in the correct order. Then, on the lines provided, write a short paragraph using the sentences and phrases to explain the process of reproduction.

_____ Within one month a human embryo is formed.

_____ The mother contributes the ovum.

_____ From four cells, the fertilized ovum divides into eight.

_____ The parents' sex cells unite into a fertilized ovum.

_____ The father contributes the sperm.

_____ After nine months, the baby is fully formed,

_____ The fertilized ovum divides into two cells,

_____ The two cells divide into four cells.

_____ Human reproduction is a many-staged process.

_____ The ovum is then fertilized.

_____ a creature that is made up of millions of cells!

_____

_____

_____

_____

_____

_____

_____

_____

Answers and explanations start on page 113.

The passage below traces the history of drug use. It follows a sequence pattern. Read the passage. Then complete the activity that follows.

Drug Use and Abuse Are Not New

If you think that the use of certain illegal drugs began in your lifetime, you are wrong. At least two drugs have been used by humans since prehistoric times.

Marijuana, for example, has been traced as far back as 2700 B.C. However, the widespread smoking of the drug didn't begin in the United States until after World War I. Fifty years later, during the 1960s, the drug was used by the "hippie generation." It was a symbol of their rejection of society's values. It is interesting that today the drug is said to have value in medicine. Some say it helps to counteract the side effects of chemotherapy. However, it is also known to impair memory and affect coordination. Many critics see marijuana as a stepping stone to harder drugs.

Opium was known to the Egyptians as early as 1500 B.C. It is derived from the juice of the poppy plant. It has been used as a painkiller since the 1700s. Over the years, doctors have prescribed it to relieve the pain of cancer, toothache, gallstones, and childbirth.

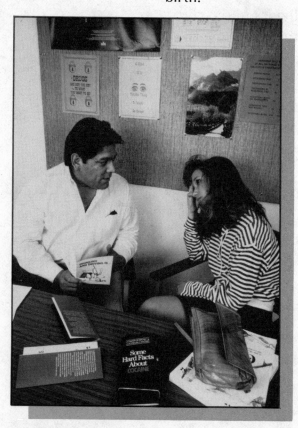

Despite its widespread uses as a painkiller, opium's addictive powers weren't suspected until its refined products, morphine and codeine, were discovered. Morphine was discovered in 1805, and codeine in 1832. During the Civil War, morphine and codeine were often injected as painkillers.

Heroin is another opium product. It was discovered in 1893. In the United States, heroin is illegal even for medical purposes. In England, however, it is legal and often prescribed as a painkiller. Though often portrayed as the most dangerous of all drugs, its effects are not that different from those of morphine, an accepted drug. However, as an addictive drug, heroin has few rivals. Heroin addiction has cut short the lives of a number of entertainers including Billie Holiday, Janis Joplin, and Jimi Hendrix.

Cocaine, another powerful drug, comes from the leaves of the coca plant. It has been grown and used in South America for hundreds of years. Coca, however, didn't become popular in Europe and the United States until the late 1800s. At that time it was used widely in tonics and beverages such as Coca-Cola. During the same time, cocaine became the first local anesthetic to be used during surgery. It was used mainly for eye operations.

Cocaine became an abused drug when doctors started prescribing it for a variety of medical problems. Widespread cocaine addiction resulted in laws being passed against its use. In the early 1900s, cocaine was removed from Coca-Cola, tonics, and other products. However, cocaine use skyrocketed to an alarming degree during the 1980s. Today it is one of the most destructive drugs.

1. Based on the passage, match the events on the left with the date listed on the right by writing the correct date in the space provided. One is done for you.

1800s a. cocaine first popularized		1900s
_____ b. cocaine use skyrockets		1960s
		2700 B.C.
_____ c. morphine discovered		1500 B.C.
_____ d. marijuana popularized		1700s
		1893
_____ e. heroin discovered		1805
_____ f. codeine discovered		1980s
		1832
_____ g. coca removed from Coca-Cola and other tonics		1800s
_____ h. date marijuana can be traced to		
_____ i. opium used by Egyptians		
_____ j. opium used as a painkiller		

2. Write *T* in the space if the statement is true, based on the information in the passage. Write *F* if it is false.

_____ **a.** Drugs have a history of being used in medicine.

_____ **b.** Some drugs are known to be addictive.

_____ **c.** Marijuana has no known medicinal properties.

_____ **d.** Most drugs are derived from growing plants.

_____ **e.** England uses heroin as a painkiller more freely than does the United States.

THINK & WRITE: Do you think that certain illegal drugs that have medicinal uses should be declared legal? Why or why not?

Answers and explanations start on page 114.

Comparison and Contrast

Comparing and contrasting—looking at similarities and differences—is part of making a decision. For example, when you decide what kind of job you want, what kind of car you want to buy, or what kind of apartment you want to rent, you are comparing and contrasting.

In making your decision, you look at advantages and disadvantages. In buying a car, for example, you must choose between a fuel-efficient two-door compact and a comfortable four-door station wagon. How do you determine the right one to buy? You'd probably consider the pluses and minuses of each. You'd compare and contrast both cars in terms of gas mileage, roominess, cost, upkeep, and so on.

The following passage below compares and contrasts city living and suburban living. As you read the passage, look for ideas about these two lifestyles that are similar and ideas that are different. Under the column *Similarities*, write things that are similar for cities and suburbs. Under the column *Differences*, write the things from the passage that are different. One is done for you.

City Living Versus Suburban Living

The U.S. population has shifted during the last century from living mainly in rural areas to living in urban areas. Urban areas include cities and suburbs. Similarities and differences exist between living in the city and living in the suburbs.

Cities and suburbs are alike in that both usually provide many recreational activities. Also, both types of communities can offer services that rural areas cannot afford. These services include regular garbage pickup, adequate fire and police protection, and public libraries. These services must be paid for, however. As a result, cities and suburbs generally have a greater tax burden than rural areas.

In spite of the similarities, many differences exist between city living and suburban living. The main difference is probably the availability of space. Suburbanites seem to take space for granted. For suburban apartment dwellers, a parking space is often only a few steps from their door. In contrast, city dwellers view space as a precious thing. They are lucky if they find a parking space after minutes of driving around looking for one.

Yard space also is plentiful in the suburbs. There, houses are usually far enough apart to allow room for a two-car garage and play areas for children. In the city, though, yard space in many parts is severely limited. Children must go to parks to play.

Sometimes city houses are so close together that it is hard to tell where one house ends and another begins. One advantage of this closeness of homes is that, in the city, people have a chance to know their neighbors. In the suburbs, for the most part, houses are so far apart that contact with neighbors is infrequent, if not difficult.

Similarities

1. Cities and suburbs provide recreational facilities.
2. _____
3. _____

Differences

Suburbanites		City Dwellers
1. parking spaces nearby	vs.	space is a precious thing
2. _____	vs.	_____
3. _____	vs.	_____
4. _____	vs.	_____
5. _____	vs.	_____

You may have noticed that the passage mentions many more differences than similarities. You should have listed these similarities: *cities and suburbs provide recreational activities; cities and suburbs provide services that rural areas cannot afford; cities and suburbs generally have a higher tax burden than rural areas.*

You should have listed these differences: *parking spaces nearby vs. space is a precious thing; yard space is plentiful vs. yard space is limited; play areas for children vs. children must go to parks; houses far apart vs. houses close together; people can get to know their neighbors vs. contact with neighbors infrequent.*

> **TIP:** These clue words indicate similarities: *and, also, likewise, in addition to, in the same way, similarly.* These clue words indicate differences: *although, however, yet, but, on the other hand, on the contrary, while, conversely, versus, in contrast to, either . . . or.*

Read the passage below, and answer the questions that follow.

Worlds Apart

For 25-year-old Pieter, who lives in Johannesburg, South Africa, being able to vote in the presidential election is no big deal. After all, the privilege to vote was part of his birthright.

However, just a few miles away on the outskirts of Johannesburg lives 25-year-old Simon. For him the right to vote in a national election is a dream. In fact, the only elections in which Simon can participate are the council elections in his all-black township.

Pieter and Simon are two men living in the same country. Yet, because of the government policy of apartheid, they live in separate worlds.

The South African government separates its people into four main groups: blacks, whites, coloreds, and Asians. Blacks, the largest group, include about 25 million people, making up 75 percent of South Africa's population. Whites, the second largest group, make up nearly 14 percent (5 million). Coloreds (those of mixed parentage) comprise 9 percent (about 3 million). Finally, Asians make up a mere 3 percent (1 million).

Although Simon is a member of the largest ethnic group, he is forced to live in a poor, all-black area, while Pieter lives in a house in the city complete with indoor plumbing and electricity.

In addition to different living conditions, Simon and Pieter receive different wages even though they work at the same mine. Simon is paid $200 a month as a laborer, compared to Pieter's $200 a week as a foreman.

Another difference between Simon and Pieter is their educational background. About 30 percent of people like Simon can read and write, contrasted to nearly 90 percent of South African whites. Trailing the literacy level of whites, but still far above that of blacks, are the Asians (69 percent) and the coloreds (62 percent).

What accounts for the high illiteracy rate among blacks in South Africa? Simon blames the nation's government. It spends an average of $186 yearly for the education of each black student compared to $1,095 for each white. The amount allotted for educating the black student also is less than the $563 spent on the Asian student and the $414 spent on the colored.

1. List three key similarities between Simon and Pieter.

a. _____

b. _____

c. _____

2. List five differences between Simon and Pieter.

Simon	**Pieter**
a. _____	**a.** _____
b. _____	**b.** _____
c. _____	**c.** _____
d. _____	**d.** _____
e. _____	**e.** _____

3. From highest to lowest, rank the groups according to total population, literacy level, and the amount of money spent on education for blacks, whites, Asians, and coloreds. One is done for you.

	Highest			Lowest
Percent of population	blacks	_____	_____	_____
Literacy level	_____	_____	_____	_____
Money spent on education	_____	_____	_____	_____

4. List five words or phrases from the passage that signal differences.

a. _____ d. _____

b. _____ e. _____

c. _____

Answers and explanations start on page 114.

Read the passage below, and complete the activity that follows.

Smoking, Thumb Sucking, and . . . Lollipops

Smoking and thumb sucking are two bad habits that are hard to break. One is an adult behavior, and the other is a childish habit. But the two have more in common than one might realize.

To begin, smoking and thumb sucking are looked upon as bad habits by many. Society generally considers smoking to be a vice. A vice is a bad habit that might be called a weakness. Thumb sucking, though, is merely looked upon by adults as undesirable behavior in children.

A second similarity between the two is that they both have bad effects on the victim's health. Smoking has long been connected with lung cancer, heart disease, and other respiratory illnesses. While thumb sucking is not nearly as hurtful to a child's health, the habit can cause crooked teeth and lisping. Parents of thumb suckers can vouch that straightening teeth is a long (and expensive) process.

The third thing in common for both is that smoking and thumb sucking are described as relaxing and calming activities. Some smokers say that smoking calms the nerves. Thumb suckers who are anxious relieve their tension by nursing their thumbs.

In spite of these similarities, obvious differences exist between smoking and thumb sucking. The chief difference is that smoking is addictive, while thumb sucking is not. The addiction-causing agent in tobacco is nicotine. This addiction makes it harder for the smoker to kick the habit. Thumb sucking, on the other hand, is usually outgrown by age two.

Another difference is that smoking is offensive (and has proved to be harmful) to nonsmokers. As a result, smoking has been limited in many public places in the United States. Thumb sucking, however, is only mildly offensive, and mainly to the parents of the children who have the habit.

Finally, some psychologists accept an interesting theory. It explains the reasons for both activities. Smoking and thumb sucking, they say, satisfy the need for oral stimulation. Perhaps this explains why many smokers who try to break the habit substitute lollipops for cigarettes and pipes.

1. The passage lists four similarities between smoking and thumb sucking. The four similarities are:

   a. _____

   b. _____

   c. _____

   d. _____

2. In the spaces below, write *S*, if the phrase applies to smoking and *T* if it applies to thumb sucking.

_____ **a.** a childish habit

_____ **b.** an adult behavior

_____ **c.** considered to be a vice by some

_____ **d.** addictive

_____ **e.** an easier habit to break

_____ **f.** inoffensive to most people

_____ **g.** life-threatening

3. What health effects of smoking are cited in the passage?_____

_____

_____

4. What effects of thumb sucking are cited in the passage?_____

_____

_____

5. The passage contains at least five "contrast" (difference) words or phrases. Write them.

_____, _____, _____, _____, _____

6. The passage contains at least three "compare" (similarity) words. Write them.

a. _____   **b.** _____   **c.** _____

7. List the four words or phrases from the passage that indicate sequence.

a. _____   **b.** _____   **c.** _____   **d.** _____

Answers and explanations start on page 114.

In the passage below, certain phrases are missing. Some of the phrases are similar to each other in meaning and some are opposite. Read the passage and fill in the blanks with the phrase that best completes the idea. Use the following phrases:

he who hesitates is lost	out of sight, out of mind
you're never too old to learn	still waters run deep
a bird in the hand is worth two in the bush	no news is good news

Friends' Advice

Connie has trouble thinking for herself. She relies on the advice of her close friends Jan and June to help her through a crisis. The only problem is that the advice Jan gives often conflicts with June's advice.

For example, when Connie's boyfriend John joined the army, she feared losing him because of the length of time they'd be separated. Jan told Connie to cheer up because the separation would make their love stronger. She said, *"Absence makes the heart grow fonder."* But June told Connie not to be a fool. "If John doesn't see you every day, he'll forget about you. Absence makes the heart go *wander.* You've heard that old saying,

"_____."

1

Weeks passed, and John didn't call or write. Connie feared the worst. Jan comforted her. She wanted to tell her friend that *what you don't know can't hurt you.* Instead, she offered these similar words of encouragement:

"_____."

2

With John gone, Connie found herself with a lot of time on her hands. She'd always wanted to learn to play the piano but figured she had gotten too old. She knew she could count on Jan to encourage her to take lessons. Upbeat Jan advised her to go ahead. She said,

"_____."

3

June, on the other hand, told her not to waste her money. Everybody knows that *"you can't teach an old dog new tricks,"* she told Connie.

Lonely because she hadn't heard from John, Connie brooded in her room. One day Dave asked her out for a date, even though she knew Dave was dating Mary. "Don't risk your relationship with John," Jan warned her. "What if he finds out? You might end up losing him. It's better to have something you can call your own than to dream about what you can't have. You know what they say:

"_____."

4

June told Connie to ignore Jan's warning. "Jan never takes a risk," she reminded Connie. "Take it from me, *nothing ventured, nothing gained.*"

Connie was confused when Dave asked her out. What should she do? She knew what Jan would say: *"You'd better look before you leap."* But Connie decided to listen to June's advice this time. She decided to take the plunge, to take a chance. Time and again she'd been told,

"_____."

5

When Jan heard about Connie's unfaithfulness, she was shocked. It wasn't like Connie. Certainly not the quiet, indecisive Connie she knew. But June said, *"You can't judge a book by its cover."* After all,

"_____."

6

7. The phrases used in the passage above are called platitudes. Platitudes are tiresome sayings or advice people sometimes give. The lesson of the above passage is that

   a. platitudes can be useful
   b. it's always best to make your own decisions
   c. never rely on the advice of friends
   d. for most platitudes, it's easy to find an opposite

8. In the passage, two pairs of platitudes are similar to one another. Write each pair.

   a. _____

   _____

   b. _____

   _____

9. Compare and contrast the natures of Jan and June. How are they alike? How are they different? Who is the "true" friend?

_____

_____

_____

THINK & WRITE: Throughout the passage, you worked with pairs of platitudes. Some were similar, and some were different. Can you think of another pair of platitudes that are either similar or opposite in meaning?

Answers and explanations start on page 114.

3 What Words Are Used?

After writers consider their audience, decide on a message, and select a pattern, they choose the best words to get their point across. In choosing their words, writers must keep the reader in mind. The words used must communicate exactly what the writer wants to say in words that the reader can understand. If a reader does not understand the words used, the message is blocked, and he or she stops reading.

Words communicate not only ideas but attitudes and feelings. These feelings can be either positive or negative. A word can arouse positive or negative feelings depending upon the association the reader has for it.

In this chapter, you will practice your skill in understanding how a writer chooses certain words to get across a particular meaning or feeling. You will learn about different uses of words.

- denotation
- connotation
- euphemisms

Denotation and Connotation

Earlier in this book, you learned that writers do not always state their meaning directly. You learned that when the writer does not spell it out for you, you must read between the lines to get the meaning. The same is true about the use of certain words. For some words you must think about what the author is implying or suggesting by the way he or she uses the words.

Many words have two levels of meaning. One level is the *literal* or dictionary definition of a word. This is called the **denotation** of the word. The other level of meaning is the implied or suggested meaning of the word. This has to do with the thoughts or feelings that the word stirs up. This level of meaning is called the **connotation** of a word.

In your experience, you have seen and heard the denotative and connotative use of words. Take for example the words *apple pie*. The two words mean literally a baked dessert consisting of two layers of pastry filled with cooked apples. This is the strict dictionary meaning of the words. The words *apple pie* have another, different meaning when they are used connotatively. They stand for traditional American values such as honesty and simplicity. Used in a sentence, the connotation is clear:

The girl next door is a perfect example of *apple pie* wholesomeness.

In the sentence, the words *apple pie* do not mean a dessert. They mean having the traditional American values of honesty and simplicity. Words can have both favorable and unfavorable connotations depending on how they have been used in the past. The words *apple pie* have a favorable connotation.

In general, the materials you read in science will use words denotatively, or literally. This is because scientific writing is objective. The scientific writer tries to keep feelings out of the writing. On the other hand, literature is more subjective. This means that the writer's feelings and attitudes often are bound up in what he or she is writing about. Therefore, you will find materials in this subject rich in the connotative use of words.

The next exercise gives you practice in understanding a word's connotation and denotation. In the sentences below, the denotations are provided for the *italicized* words. Decide whether or not the meaning is favorable or unfavorable, then supply the correct connotation on the line. The first is done for you.

Chicago's magnet schools are successful mainly because they attract the *cream* of Chicago's public school students.

WORD: cream
DENOTATION: the yellowish part of milk containing from 18 to about 40 percent butterfat
CONNOTATION IN SENTENCE: favorable
MEANING IN SENTENCE: the choicest part, the best

Only a week after she had driven the car, Brenda learned that it was a *lemon.*

WORD: lemon
DENOTATION: a pale yellow, oblong acid fruit of the citrus family
CONNOTATION IN SENTENCE: favorable   unfavorable   (*circle one*)

MEANING IN SENTENCE: _____

The governor awarded his campaign aides jobs, free season tickets to football games, and other *plums.*

WORD: plum
DENOTATION: an oval, smooth-skinned fruit containing oblong seeds
CONNOTATION IN SENTENCE: favorable   unfavorable (*circle one*)

MEANING IN SENTENCE: _____

Were you able to determine the connotations for the words above? For *lemon*, the connotation is unfavorable; for its meaning, you should have written something like a *defective automobile*. For *plum*, the connotation is favorable; you should have written *something desirable given in return for a favor*, or something similar.

> **TIP:** When trying to determine the connotation of a word, think about the feeling the word stirs in you. Try to recall similar ways in which you have heard the words used in the past.

Read the following essay by Sydney J. Harris about connotations, and complete the activity that follows.

A Writer Needs an Ear for Words

While reading the entries as one of the judges in a collegiate writing contest, I was reminded of Mark Twain's annoyed remark that "the difference between the right word and the *almost* right word is the difference between lightning and the lightning bug."

Most persons—and this includes aspiring[1] writers—simply fail to recognize that there are very few true synonyms in the language, no matter what the dictionary may insist.

The dictionary, for instance, gives "devour" as a synonym for "eat." But no woman would care to have it said of her that she "devoured her dinner," which sounds more like an animal than a human. . . .

Again, a woman's eyes may "glow" with affection, but they do not "glitter," although the two words are roughly synonymous. Eyes "glitter" with greed or contempt, but they "glow" with love or compassion.

Distinguishing between two words that seem to mean the same, but have different colors and shapes and suggestions—this is essential to the art of writing, and also of speaking. The dictionary can tell you only what a word points to; it cannot tell you what it feels like.

An interesting example is the word "fat." The unabridged[2] dictionary gives as synonyms: fleshy, plump, corpulent, obese, stocky, portly, tubby, thick, among others.

Obviously, different people are fat in different ways—a woman may be "fleshy," but a man is "portly." "Obese" carries the connotation of glandular sickness. "Stocky" involves size as well as shape. We speak of a "plump" or "tubby" baby, but nobody would call him "corpulent."

---

[1]*aspiring*—wishing to become
[2]*unabridged*—complete

The same is true of hundreds of words which only superficially[3] resemble one another. "Unspeakable" in the dictionary means the same as "unutterable"—but the former is always used to mean something base or vile, while the latter usually means some rapturous or divine thought or emotion.

The right word is as important to the writer as the right note to the composer or the right line to the painter.

Hemingway's prose is so compelling . . . precisely because he always [knew] the right word to capture the essence of a situation or the feel of a person. A writer needs an "ear" as much as a musician does.

And without this ear, he is lost and groping in a forest of words, where all the trees look much alike.

---

[3] *superficially*—on the surface

1. Based on what you read in the passage above, read each sentence and underline the word that suggests the appropriate connotation.

   a. Mrs. Hoover (*ate, devoured*) her dinner as if it were her last.

   b. The look in the German shepherd's eyes made me feel as if I would be (*eaten, devoured*).

   c. Whenever Constance is in love, her (*glowing, glittering*) eyes tell the story.

   d. The crooks' eyes (*glowed, glittered*) with greed as they divided the $20 thousand.

   e. (*Obesity, Fatness*) is sometimes linked to an underactive thyroid gland.

   f. The toddler was quite (*stocky, plump*) for a nine-month-old.

   g. My delight at hearing you play at the recital was (*unspeakable, unutterable*).

   h. My thoughts about the violence and obscenity of the movie are (*unspeakable, unutterable*).

2. Which sentence bests states the main idea in the essay?

   a. Most words have only one meaning.
   b. Since words have shades of meaning, writers must be careful to use them appropriately.
   c. Ernest Hemingway always knew precisely the connotations of the words he used.
   d. Many people think that not enough words exist in the English language to express their ideas accurately.

Answers and explanations start on page 115.

As you just learned, words can have favorable or unfavorable connotations. Sometimes people substitute an agreeable word or expression for one that is offensive. These more pleasant-sounding words are called *euphemisms*.

Read the passage below, and complete the activity that follows.

What's in a Name?

Are you happy with your job title? Does it reflect what you actually do? If you could change it, would you? These questions were asked of a group of workers during a survey of job titles. The survey was conducted by job counselors. The answers indicated that most employees would change their job title to reflect their job responsibilities.

Many people agreed that today jobs have become more specialized. This has led to a need for more accurate job descriptions. But does this need to change titles indicate status consciousness or a desire for more accurate descriptions?

At one time, a person who styled hair was called a beautician. The job included shampooing, conditioning, cutting, and styling. Today, the word *beautician* is being replaced by *hair stylist* or *hair designer*, even though the duties remain the same as in the past.

Similarly, janitors have become *maintenance engineers*. Garbage collectors have become *sanitation engineers*. Undertakers have become *funeral directors* or *morticians*. Homemakers have become *domestic engineers*!

Apparently these new titles carry more favorable connotations. Job counselors argue that the more fancy titles add higher status to the positions. At least in the workers' eyes they do. As a result, the workers feel better about their work.

It seems, however, that what the public thinks plays a big part in the desire for more fancy titles. After all, what others think of you has much to do with your opinion of yourself. If that is true, William Shakespeare was wrong. A rose by any other name does *not* smell as sweet—it could smell sweeter.

1. In the spaces below, write in the word from the passage that has a more favorable connotation.

Less favorable	More favorable
a. beautician	_____
b. janitor	_____
c. garbage collector	_____
d. undertaker	_____
e. homemaker	_____

2. Of the following statements, which is implied and not stated directly by the passage?

   a. What others think of you helps determine what you think of yourself.
   b. American workers are more status conscious than other workers.
   c. Those who are secure in themselves do not need a title change to bring prestige.
   d. White collar workers command more respect than blue collar workers.

THINK & WRITE: You want a new shopping area built in your town, and you want other citizens to be willing to pay more in taxes for it. What are five words you would use to describe the new area that you want others to support? _____

_____

Now switch positions. You don't want to pay taxes for the new shopping area. Use five *unfavorable* words to describe the new shopping area negatively. _____

_____

Answers and explanations start on page 115.

Skill Review

Directions: In this exercise you will have a chance to practice many of the skills you have learned so far. Read the introduction and selection below. Then complete the activities that follow.

The following selection is an adaptation of a work by Mark Twain, one of America's greatest humorists and writers. Twain was an anti-imperialist. An anti-imperialist is a person who is against one country using force to acquire more territory. The work is most probably based on Twain's feelings about the Spanish-American War, which took place in 1898. After the war, the United States gained control of several territories that formerly were under Spanish control. The work was considered to be controversial for its time. Twain requested that it be published only after his death. He died in 1910; the work was published in 1923.

The War Prayer

Part I

It was a time of great excitement. The country was at war. The drums were beating. The bands were playing. Old and young alike joined in the celebration with toy pistols and firecrackers. From every balcony and rooftop flags flew.

Every day young volunteers marched proudly down the street showing off their fine uniforms. Proud mothers and fathers and sisters and sweethearts cheered them on as they passed by.

Every night mass meetings were held where people listened to soul-stirring speeches. At points during the speeches they applauded, tears running down their cheeks.

In churches all over town, pastors preached devotion to the flag and country and prayed for God's help in winning the war.

The war fever was so high that those who disapproved of the war kept their opinions to themselves because they feared for their personal safety.

Part II

Sunday morning came. The next day the soldiers would leave for the battlefront. The church was filled. The young volunteers were there. On their faces was the vision of being on the front line of victory. They had dreams of the surrender and saw themselves coming home to a hero's welcome. With the volunteers sat their loved ones, proud, happy and envied by the neighbors who had no sons or brothers to send to the field of honor.

The service began. A war chapter was read, followed by a musical selection that shook the building. The pastor began his prayer.

> Our Father, please watch over our noble young soldiers and help, comfort, and encourage them in their patriotic work. Bless them. Shield them in the day of battle and the hour of danger. Make them strong and confident. Make them victorious in the bloody battle. Help them to destroy the enemy. Give to them and their country indestructible honor and glory!

As the pastor spoke, an elderly stranger clothed in a long robe entered the church and walked slowly and quietly up the main aisle. His eyes were fixed on the minister, and all eyes followed him with wonder. When he finally reached the pulpit, he stood at the preacher's side. The preacher, unaware of his presence, continued his Morning Prayer. He ended with these words:

> Bless our weapons. Grant us the victory, O Lord our God, Father and Protector of our land and flag.

The stranger touched his arm and motioned for the pastor to step aside. When the startled minister did, the stranger took his place. He surveyed the spellbound audience and then spoke in a deep voice,

> I came with a message from the Almighty God! He has heard the prayer of your shepherd and will grant it if such be your desire after I have explained its full meaning.

> It is like the many prayers of men in that it asks for more than he who speaks is aware of, unless he stops and thinks. Your shepherd has prayed his prayer. But has he paused and taken thought? Is it one prayer? No, it is two. One is spoken; the other not. Both prayers have reached the Almighty.

> Ponder this and keep it in mind. If you would ask for a blessing upon yourself, beware because without intending to, you may be asking for a curse upon a neighbor at the same time.

If you pray for the blessing of rain upon your crop that needs it, you may be praying for a curse upon some neighbor's crop, which may not need rain and might be damaged by it.

You have heard your servant's prayer, the *spoken* part of it. I was sent here to explain the *other* part of it, that part which the pastor and also you spoke in your hearts and intensely prayed for silently and ignorantly and unthinkingly. When you have prayed for victory you have prayed for many unmentioned results that follow victory.

When you prayed for victory, what you really have prayed for is to have children, wives, and mothers lose their fathers, husbands, and sons in a bloody battle.

When you have prayed for victory, you have actually prayed for homes to be destroyed and for people to go without food. Think about it!

As the messenger left the pulpit and started down the aisle, one man puzzled by the messenger's speech uttered, "Is he crazy?"

1. An appropriate title for this selection might be

   a. All's Well That Ends Well
   b. War Is Hell
   c. A Mixed Blessing
   d. In the Pulpit

2. Arrange the following events in time order. Use the number 1 for the first event that occurred, 2 for the second, and so on.

   _____ **a.** An elderly man walked up the aisle to the pulpit.

   _____ **b.** A war chapter was read, and a musical selection was given.

   _____ **c.** The pastor began praying for victory in war.

   _____ **d.** The stranger took the minister's place in the pulpit.

   _____ **e.** The elderly stranger motioned the pastor to step aside.

   _____ **f.** Someone in the audience questioned the stranger's sanity.

   _____ **g.** The stranger spoke to the congregation.

3. The young men in uniform are held in high esteem because

   _____

   _____

4. Compare the mood in the church *before* and *during* the stranger's speech by writing one descriptive word.

Before: During:

_____   _____

5. Why do you think only a few people spoke openly against the war?

_____

_____

6. In his prayer, what is the pastor asking for? _____

_____

Why does Twain think that this request is not in keeping with the role of a pastor? _____

_____

_____

7. Based on what the stranger says, what can you infer from the "War Prayer?"

   a. To pray for victory in war is against the will of God.
   b. Only patriotic people should be allowed to fight for their country.
   c. War brings out the best in human nature.
   d. In wartime, God is on the side of the righteous.

8. From the content of the "War Prayer," you probably can conclude that Mark Twain withheld the poem from publication during his lifetime because _____

_____

_____

9. At the end of the stranger's message, a man questions the messenger's sanity. What does this suggest about society's attitude toward people who do not "go along to get along?"

_____

_____

10. During the Vietnam War, there was an outpouring of protest against what many Americans considered to be an unfair war. Many religious leaders openly opposed the war. Why do you think they reacted differently than did the pastor described in Twain's poem?

_____

_____

_____

THINK & WRITE: Can you think of a situation in which a blessing for you might have been a curse for someone else?

Answers and explanations start on page 115.

2 Critical-Thinking Skills

When you think critically about what you read, you look beneath the surface for hidden meanings or views the author holds. By going a step beyond the words that you read, you decide if a conclusion is based on fact or opinion. In this section, you will read different forms of writing. In addition to weighing conclusions, you will understand the role values play in writing. You will see how writers slant messages based on their personal feelings. You will look at the patterns of logic they use to see how effective they are in proving a point. Finally, you will learn how writers use certain methods to influence readers to think, feel, or act the way the writer wants them to.

4 How Sound Is the Reasoning?

Writers have a responsibility to state their ideas logically. The thinking behind what they write must be sensible. When a message is sound, the reader or listener cannot easily dismiss what the writer is saying. Then the reader can't "poke holes" in the writer's argument.

On the other hand, if the writer relies on half-truths or misuses words, the message that comes out is distorted. Unless the reader is careful, he or she will believe and accept untrue or illogical ideas.

When you read textbooks, they have been carefully written, and efforts have been made to weed out errors in reasoning. However, you are exposed every day to errors in logic when you listen to political speeches, advertising claims, and other methods of communication that try to persuade you to act or think in a certain way.

In this chapter, you will practice your skills in the following areas:

- identifying invalid conclusions
- distinguishing among fact, opinion, and hypothesis
- identifying stereotypes
- identifying values and beliefs

Invalid Conclusions

When people come to a conclusion without having all the facts needed to back it up, or interpret facts in the wrong way, they are making an *invalid conclusion*. Invalid conclusions are mistakes in reasoning.

For example, if you spotted an elderly man searching through trash cans in the cold, you might conclude that he is a homeless person looking for food. But do you have all of the facts needed to draw this conclusion? The man could have a home and a loving family who is looking for him. He might be confused, or he might be a victim of Alzheimer's disease, which affects memory and behavior. Or he could be looking for returnable aluminum cans to redeem for deposit. To draw a conclusion about the man's situation, you need to have all of the facts and must consider them carefully.

Read the dialogue below to determine why the conclusion reached is invalid.

18-YEAR-OLD-DAUGHTER: Sorry I'm late, Mom. But on the way home, I had a flat tire.

MOTHER: I'll bet you did! The last movie ended three hours ago. How long does it take to fix a flat tire? Stop trying to pull the wool over my eyes. . . . Tell me the truth.

DAUGHTER: Mom, I am telling you the truth. I had a flat tire and was stranded on Route 43 . . .

MOTHER: Don't bother trying to explain. I know where you were. You went to that after-hours hangout—Harley's. That's where your Dad found your older sister when she didn't come home at a decent hour.

The mother's conclusion is invalid because

   a. the daughter's excuse is airtight
   b. she has no proof to refute the daughter's explanation
   c. parents never give their children the benefit of the doubt

If you chose b, you chose the correct reason that explains why the mother's reasoning is faulty and the conclusion is invalid. The mother has no proof that her daughter did not have a flat tire. Moreover, it is faulty reasoning to assume that one person is guilty of an action because another person was guilty of the same action. The mother's conclusion *could* be correct, but since she lacks proof, she can't be certain.

A Heart Gives Out

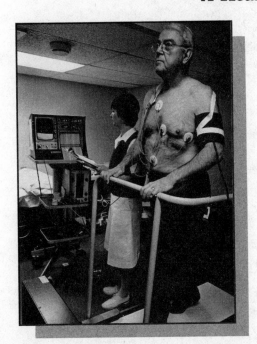

On Wednesday November 25, 1987, one of the nation's most dynamic and tenacious political leaders died. Harold Washington, the first black mayor of Chicago, became the victim of the nation's number one killer—sudden cardiac arrest.

Sudden cardiac death happens approximately 1,200 times daily. This means that about 438,000 people die each year, or roughly one death occurs every 72 seconds.

According to medical experts, in one out of three cases, the first sign of heart disease is the sudden attack itself. Unfortunately, death almost always follows.

Mayor Washington was such a case, despite the state-of-the-art medical care used to revive him. He was reportedly 100 pounds overweight and had a history of heavy smoking.

According to Dr. Antonio Senat, the mayor's personal doctor, he also suffered from high cholesterol levels and high blood pressure. He was referred to as "the mayor with the big heart." Autopsy results proved just how accurate the description was. His heart had swollen to over twice its normal size. As a result, the mayor's coronary arteries were severely blocked. This blockage can be compared to a rusty pump trying to force water through a clamped hose. Simply put, Mayor Washington's heart gave out after years of pumping against increased resistance.

Medical experts, friends, and co-workers questioned whether the mayor had noticed symptoms of his heart disease. It seems certain that no one really knew for sure. But the mayor's doctor said that his patient had been told that he was in the high-risk group.

According to Dr. Robert S. Elliot, a cardiac expert, high blood pressure alone doubles the risk of heart attacks. (Blacks develop high blood pressure twice as often as whites. They die from it three times as often.) People who smoke or have high cholesterol levels carry a risk that is eight times higher. Those who have high blood pressure, smoke, *and* have a high cholesterol level carry a risk that is up to twelve times higher. For those who have all three of these risk factors and are obese, the risk doubles again. So Mayor Washington's risk was twenty-four times greater than the average!

The mayor's personal doctor thinks that, in addition to his heart problems, his patient may have been suffering from the stress of running the third largest city in the United States.

"He was a workaholic . . .," the doctor recalls, "a man intensely focused on what he wanted to accomplish."

The doctor added that the stress of the constant fighting in City Hall helped to run the mayor down. The "council wars" that marked his first four years in office added greatly to the mayor's failing health.

Indeed, had it not been for the stress brought on by the opposition aldermen's efforts to block Mayor Washington, "the mayor who loved Chicago more than he loved himself" might still be alive and well today.

1. Which of the following is an invalid conclusion contained in the passage?

   a. Mayor Harold Washington was the victim of an acute heart attack.
   b. Sudden cardiac death occurs about 1,200 times a day in the United States.
   c. About every 72 seconds, one in three people in the nation dies because of heart failure.
   d. Mayor Washington's sudden heart attack was directly caused by the ongoing fighting in City Hall.

2. Write *V* in the space provided if the statement is a valid conclusion based on the information provided and *I* if it is invalid.

   _____ **a.** If a person with high blood pressure and high cholesterol does not get regular checkups, that person will die of a heart attack.

   _____ **b.** If you smoke, have high cholesterol and high blood pressure, and are white, your chance of survival from a heart attack is greater than that of a black person with the same health profile.

   _____ **c.** Losing weight, lowering cholesterol intake, and not smoking can reduce the risk of suffering a heart attack.

   _____ **d.** Had the mayor not loved Chicago so much, he might be alive today.

   _____ **e.** Nothing can be done to reduce the risk of a cardiac arrest if a person is in the high-risk category.

3. The term *state-of-the-art* means

   a. outdated
   b. modern
   c. experimental
   d. provided for by state taxes

Answers and explanations start on page 115.

In the following excerpt from *Twelve Angry Men*, jurors (identified by numbers) discuss the fate of a young man who has been accused of murder. Read the excerpt. Then complete the activity that follows.

EIGHT: There were eleven votes for guilty. It's not easy for me to raise my hand and send a boy off to die without talking about it first.

SEVEN: Who says it's easy for me?

EIGHT: No one.

SEVEN: What, just because I voted fast? I think the guy's guilty. You couldn't change my mind if you talked for a hundred years.

EIGHT: I don't want to change your mind, I just want to talk for a while. Look, this boy's been kicked around all his life. You know, living in a slum, his mother dead since he was nine. That's not a very good head start. He's a tough angry kid. You know why slum kids get that way. Because we knock 'em on the head once a day, every day. I think we owe him a few words that's all.

[*He looks around the table. Some of them look back coldly. Some cannot look at him. Only NINE nods slowly. TWELVE doodles steadily. FOUR begins to comb his hair.*]

TEN: I don't mind telling you this, mister. We don't owe him a thing. He got a fair trial, didn't he? You know what that trial cost? He's lucky he got it. Look, we're all grownups here. You're not going to tell us that we're supposed to believe him, knowing what he is. I've lived among 'em all my life. You can't believe a word they say. You know that.

NINE: [*to TEN very slowly*] I don't know that. What a terrible thing for a man to believe. Since when is dishonesty a group characteristic? You have no monopoly on the truth.

THREE: [*interrupting*] All right. It's not Sunday. We don't need a sermon.

NINE: What this man says is very dangerous.

[*EIGHT puts his hand on NINE's arm and stops him. Somehow his touch and gentle expression calm the old man. He draws a deep breath and relaxes.*]

FOUR: I don't see any need for arguing like this. I think we ought to be able to behave like gentlemen.

SEVEN: Right!

FOUR: If we're going to discuss this case, let's discuss the facts.

FOREMAN: I think that's a good point. We have a job to do. Let's do it.

1. Which of the following is an invalid conclusion suggested in the passage?

   a. Getting knocked in the head is a daily occurrence for teenagers who live in disadvantaged areas.
   b. Teenagers living in urban areas have many obstacles to overcome.
   c. Teenagers from upper middle class families usually aren't abused.
   d. To develop socially and emotionally, children need the love and support of both parents.

2. The conclusion you checked above is invalid because

   a. it goes against the facts presented in the play
   b. not enough facts are given to support it
   c. it has no bearing on the verdict that has to be given
   d. it is true only in a limited number of cases

3. Which juror appears to show the most concern for the defendant?

   _____

4. Which juror appears to show the least concern?

   _____

Answers and explanations start on page 116.

You have practiced identifying faulty logic in a written passage. In this lesson, you will demonstrate your ability to recognize invalid conclusions based on illustrated material. You probably have seen illustrated materials such as graphs and charts used to make a point. In many instances, though, it is not the information presented in the visuals that is questionable. It is the way the information is interpreted that causes errors in reasoning.

Based on the information presented in the graph, decide whether or not each of the following statements is a valid or invalid conclusion. If the statement is valid, write *V* on the line. If it is invalid, write *I*.

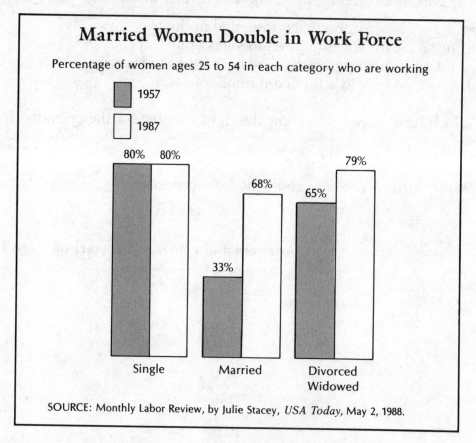

Married Women Double in Work Force

Percentage of women ages 25 to 54 in each category who are working

☐ 1957
☐ 1987

	Single	Married	Divorced Widowed
1957	80%	33%	65%
1987	80%	68%	79%

SOURCE: Monthly Labor Review, by Julie Stacey, *USA Today*, May 2, 1988.

_____ **1.** The graph shows that in 1987 more than twice as many married women had jobs as they had in 1957.

_____ **2.** More married women are working because they want to prove that they can "do it all."

_____ **3.** The trend among the number of single women in the work force has remained the same within a 30-year period.

_____ **4.** More divorced women are working now than 30 years ago because alimony and child support payments are unenforceable.

_____ **5.** In 1987, 11 percent more divorced and widowed women were working than married women.

_____ **6.** The United States has become primarily a two-income-family nation within the past 30 years.

Answers and explanations start on page 116.

Values

What is important to you? Is it owning a home or being the best dressed among your friends? Is it being honest or withholding the truth to protect yourself or someone else? Is it working on a job paying "big bucks" that you despise or having a job that you love but that pays little money? Your answers to these questions reflect your values.

A *value* represents a belief about what is important in life. It influences the decisions that we make. Values can be based on three things:

- standards of right and wrong as determined by religion or upbringing
- cultural needs or customs
- individual taste

Not only are your values influenced by what you approve of, but they also are influenced by the values of others such as your parents, teachers, friends, or religious leaders. In other words, your values are the result of many influences in your life.

In the situation below, determine what value is more important and write the appropriate words in the blanks provided.

A model refuses to advertise a product that she knows doesn't live up to its claims in spite of being offered $50,000 to do it. The model probably values _____ over _____.

You should have written that the model values *honesty* or *integrity* over *money,* or something similar. In this example, the values are clear-cut. In other things you read, the values clash may be less clearly drawn.

As you read the following story by Juan A. A. Sedillo, consider the kinds of values being shown. Then answer the questions that follow.

The Gentleman of Rio en Medio

It took months of negotiation to come to an understanding with the old man. He was in no hurry. What he had the most of was time. He lived up in Rio en Medio, where his people had been for hundreds of years. He tilled the same land they had tilled. His house was small and wretched, but quaint. The little creek ran through his land. His orchard was gnarled[1] and beautiful.

The day of the sale he came into the office. His coat was old, green and faded. I thought of Senator Catron, who had been such a power with these people up there in the mountains. Perhaps it was one of his old Prince Alberts[2]. He also wore gloves. They were old and torn and his fingertips showed through them. He carried a cane, but it was only a skeleton of a worn-out umbrella. Behind him walked one of his innumerable[3] kin—a dark young man with eyes like a gazelle[4].

The old man bowed to all of us in the room. Then he removed his hat and gloves, slowly and carefully. Chaplin once did that in a picture, in a bank—he was the janitor. Then he handed his things to the boy, who stood obediently behind the old man's chair.

There was a great deal of conversation, about rain and about his family. He was very proud of his large family. Finally we got down to business. Yes, he would sell, as he had agreed, for twelve hundred dollars, in cash. We would buy, the money was ready. "Don Anselmo," I said to him in Spanish, "we have made a discovery. You remember that we sent that surveyor, that engineer, up there to survey your land so as to make the deed. Well, he finds that you own more than eight acres. He tells us that your land extends across the river and that you own almost twice as much as you thought." He didn't know that. "And now, Don Anselmo," I added, "these Americans are *buena gente*, they are good people, and they are willing to pay you for the additional land as well, at the same rate per acre, so that instead of twelve hundred dollars you will get almost twice as much, and the money is here for you."

The old man hung his head for a moment in thought. Then he stood up and stared at me. "Friend," he said, "I do not like to have you speak to me in that manner." I kept still and let him have his say. "I know these Americans are good people, and that is why I have agreed to sell my house to them. But I do not care to be insulted. I have agreed to sell my house and land for twelve hundred dollars and that is the price."

---

[1]gnarled--twisted
[2]Prince Albert—a long doublebreasted coat
[3]innumerable—many
[4]gazelle—a deerlike animal

I argued with him but it was useless. Finally he signed the deed and took the money but refused to take more than the amount agreed upon. Then he shook hands all around, put on his ragged gloves, took his stick and walked out with the boy behind him.

A month later my friends had moved into Rio en Medio. They had replastered the old adobe house, pruned the trees, patched the fence, and moved in for the summer. One day they came back to the office to complain. The children of the village were overrunning their property. They came every day and played under the trees, built little play fences around them, and took blossoms. When they were spoken to they only laughed and talked back good-naturedly in Spanish.

I sent a messenger up to the mountains for Don Anselmo. It took a week to arrange another meeting. When he arrived he repeated his previous preliminary[5] performance. He wore the same faded cutaway, carried the same stick and was accompanied by the boy again. He shook hands all around, sat down with the boy behind his chair, and talked about the weather. Finally I broached[6] the subject. "Don Anselmo, about the ranch you sold to these people. They are good people and want to be your friends and neighbors always. When you sold to them you signed a document, a deed, and in that deed you agreed to several things. One thing was that they were to have the complete possession of the property. Now, Don Anselmo, it seems that every day the children of the village overrun the orchard and spend most of their time there. We would like to know if you, as the most respected man in the village, could not stop them from doing so in order that these people may enjoy their new home more in peace."

Don Anselmo stood up. "We have all learned to love these Americans," he said, "because they are good people and good neighbors. I sold them my property because I knew they were good people, but I did not sell them the trees in the orchard."

This was bad. "Don Anselmo," I pleaded, "when one signs a deed and sells real property one sells also everything that grows on the land, and those trees, every one of them, are on the land inside the boundaries of what you sold."

"Yes, I admit that," he said. "You know," he added. "I am the oldest man in the village. Almost everyone there is my relative and all the children of Rio en Medio are my *sobrinos* and *nietos*, my descendants. Every time a child has been born in Rio en Medio since I took possession of that house from my mother I have planted a tree for that child. The trees in that orchard are not mine, Senor, they belong to the children of the village. Every person in Rio en Medio born since the railroad came to Santa Fe owns a tree in that orchard. I did not

---

[5]preliminary—coming before
[6]broached—brought up in conversation

sell the trees because I could not. They are not mine."

There was nothing we could do. Legally we owned the trees but the old man had been so generous, refusing what amounted to a fortune for him. It took most of the following winter to buy the trees, individually, from the descendants of Don Anselmo in the valley of Rio en Medio.

1. According to the story, which of the following summarizes Don Anselmo's values?

   a. Don Anselmo is more concerned about money than he is about family.
   b. Don Anselmo is kind only to people born in Mexico.
   c. Don Anselmo is a man of his word who values family more than money.
   d. Don Anselmo is a man who can't be trusted because he betrayed the Americans as well as his family.

2. Write two sentences directly from the story that show that Don Anselmo is a mannerly, dignified man.

   a. _____

   _____

   b. _____

   _____

3. What do the Americans finally do to demonstrate that they respect the generosity and family loyalty of Don Anselmo?

   _____

   _____

4. What legal action could the Americans have taken to stop their property from being overrun?

   _____

   _____

5. Which of the following statements summarizes why the Americans are surprised by Don Anselmo's value system?

   a. In the United States, a seller gets as much money as possible for his or her property.
   b. The Americans thought that perhaps Don Anselmo didn't really own the land and that he was trying to trick them.
   c. The Americans are surprised because American children do not value playing under trees, building fences, and picking flowers.
   d. The "gentleman" is rich and does not need to take advantage of their generosity.

6. The story is titled "Gentleman of Rio en Medio" because the main character

   a. is a man who wanted to sell his property
   b. does not value land in the forest
   c. is polite, loyal, considerate, and respected
   d. is shrewd, calculating, inflexible, and stubborn

7. Don Anselmo's attitude toward property and ownership is most similar to the attitude of which people who believe that land can belong to no man?

   a. Europeans
   b. Native American Indians
   c. Japanese

Answers and explanations start on page 116.

Read the passage below, then answer the questions that follow.

Is the "Right to Die" a Wrong Idea?

Early in 1988, a doctor published an essay. In it he described giving an overdose of morphine to a young woman. She was dying and in severe pain. The overdose killed the woman in five minutes.

In California a man admitted that he had helped his AIDS-stricken friend end his life.

A few years earlier, an elderly man had been jailed because he pulled the plug on his wife's life-support system. She died immediately.

In still another case, the family of a young woman got a court order to disconnect her life-support system. She lay in a coma for several months before her death.

Are these people heroes or criminals? Are the parents of the young woman who lay in a coma for several months killers? Or are they people who have compassion for their loved ones?

Situations such as these have brought the issue of mercy killing to the public eye. In fact, some supporters of mercy killing have proposed letting the voters decide whether doctors should help dying patients end their lives when they ask for such assistance. One proposal requires that two doctors give their consent to disconnect a life-support system or to use some other method of putting a patient out of misery. However, critics from around the nation have opposed this proposal. They questioned giving doctors the right to "play God." Yet, supporters of mercy killing point out that some European nations do permit mercy killings. They consider them to be acts of charity.

Closely connected to mercy killings is the moral question of keeping elderly patients alive on life-support systems at great cost. Estimates in 1988 revealed that nationwide, about 10,000 dying elderly patients are kept alive on such systems. The cost is $1 billion dollars a year. Critics of this practice charge that money spent on prolonging the lives of the terminally ill should be spent differently. It should be spent on saving the lives of the many Americans who can't pay for adequate medical care.

1. The Netherlands spends many dollars per year on health care. The number of terminally ill patients kept on life-support systems there is extremely low compared to the number in the United States. The Dutch spend their medical dollars on providing medical care for the living. In this case a value is decided by

   a. standards of right and wrong as determined by religion
   b. needs of the culture
   c. individual taste

2. Critics who question the doctor's right to "pull the plug" on terminally ill patients apparently base their view on

   a. standards of right and wrong as determined by religion
   b. needs of the culture
   c. individual taste

Answers and explanations start on page 117.

A recent survey of 509 lawyers in 1988 found that more than half believe that the administration of a lethal (deadly) injection to terminally ill patients should be legal. The following pie graph shows the results of the survey. Study the graph and answer the questions that follow.

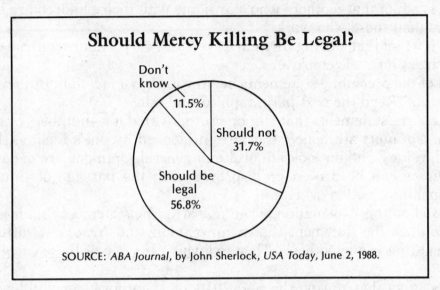

Should Mercy Killing Be Legal?

Don't know
11.5%

Should not
31.7%

Should be legal
56.8%

SOURCE: *ABA Journal*, by John Sherlock, *USA Today*, June 2, 1988.

1. The information in the survey may not be a reliable representation of lawyers' opinions because it is not clear

   a. whether a majority opinion is shown
   b. whether they represent a geographic cross-section of the United States
   c. how long they have been practicing law

2. The graph shows that even if the percentage of lawyers who responded "Don't Know" is added to the percentage that opposes legalizing mercy killing, the majority of the 509 lawyers

   a. approve legalizing mercy killing
   b. oppose legalizing mercy killing
   c. have no clear-cut position on the issue

3. In deciding whether or not to legalize mercy killing, the opinion of which type of lawyer would probably carry the least weight?

   a. specialist in criminal law
   b. specialist in civil law
   c. specialist in real estate law

THINK & WRITE: Should doctors have the right to help terminally ill patients die?

Answers and explanations start on page 117.

Fact, Opinion, and Hypothesis

"It is a fact that the heads of most households work."

"It is a fact that mothers who stay home with their children are better mothers than those who work."

"It is a fact that, during the year 2010, most corporations will have day-care centers for their employees.

All of the preceding statements begin with *It is a fact that*. But are they really facts? Read the next paragraph to find out.

Facts are statements that can be proved with data—numbers or information. **Opinions** are beliefs that are influenced by one's feelings, background, values, and outlook about life in general. Opinions are debatable. **Hypotheses** can be proved or disproved with the passage of time and additional information or data.

Based on this explanation, write *fact* after the statement that is a fact, *opinion* after the statement that is an opinion, and *hypothesis* after the statement that is a hypothesis. Then tell why it fits one of these categories.

1. It is a fact that, during the year 2010, most corporations will have

   day-care centers for their employees. _____

   Reason: _____

2. It is a fact that mothers who stay home with their children are better

   mothers than those who work. _____

   Reason: _____

3. It is a fact that the heads of most households work. _____

   Reason: _____

Based on the explanation provided above, you should have concluded that:

- Statement 1 is a *hypothesis* because it is not known now but can be proved (or disproved) after the passage of time (during the year 2010). After the year 2010 passes, you could get information about the number of large corporations that provide day-care facilities for their employees.

- Statement 2 is an *opinion* because it is based on a person's feelings. What makes one mother "better" than another is a matter of opinion.

- Statement 3 is a *fact* because it can be proved by studying data about the occupational status of heads of households.

You may have noticed that all of the statements at the beginning of this topic begin with the words *It is a fact*. However, not all of the statements are facts. Other introductory phrases that are used often but that do not necessarily indicate facts are: *the truth is; as a matter of fact; the point is;* and *in fact*.

> **T**IP: The following phrases indicate an opinion: *in my opinion; I think/believe/feel;* and *should be*. Also, emotionally charged words like *evil, beautiful,* and *wonderful* indicate that an opinion is being expressed.

The title of the anecdote below introduces the term *yankee gringo*, which is used in Latin America to describe a foreigner, especially one of English or U.S. origin. Read the anecdote and answer the questions that follow.

Curious Tourist, Yankee Gringo

The train is traveling from Los Mochis to Chihuahua, a route that covers over 415 miles of Mexico. The passengers riding the Copper Canyon Railroad are taking in the scenic route to the Topolobampo Bay on the Sea of Cortez.

Sarah and Sid Johnson, Americans from Cincinnati, Ohio, are touring Mexico by train to learn the culture of the natives. Along the way, Sid is reading *The Old Gringo* by Carlos Fuentes and is studying Mexican cuisine. Dressed in travel gear (shorts and bikini top), Sarah is taking a "crash course" in Spanish by reading *El Dia*.

Just across the aisle in the tourist-class compartment sit Julia and Miguel Garcia-Marquez. On their first-anniversary holiday, they are going to meet relatives near the popular Puerto al Pacifico Resort.

Julia and Miguel snicker softly as the Johnsons hide their money belt from their companions in the train car. Julia points out to her husband the diamond engagement ring and wedding band that Sarah wears on her left hand and compares them to her own simple gold band to her husband. She refers to the couple as "Yankee gringo" as the train glides through the twilight.

Sarah, speaking in slow and halting Spanish, addresses Julia: "Do you have change for *cincuenta mil pesos*?[1] I want to have coins for the poor beggar boys at the station. They are so cute—and needy." Miguel, in clear American English, replies, "With the current rate of inflation, those darling kids need dollar bills." Adds Julia, "If you Americans really wanted to help those 'cute and needy' kids, you'd give their parents jobs in your country."

---

[1] 500 pesos

1. Which of the following statements is a hypothesis that may be based on the passage?

   a. If their parents had jobs, many Mexican children would not have to beg American tourists for money.
   b. Mexicans do not earn enough money to support their families.
   c. To improve living conditions in Mexico, more foreign aid is needed.
   d. As soon as Julia and Miguel save more money, they will go to the United States.

2. Write *F* before the statements that are facts and *O* by those that are opinions.

   _____ a. Mexican food is tastier than Puerto Rican food.
   _____ b. Julia and Miguel have been married for a year.
   _____ c. Sarah and Sid are riding in the tourist-class car of the train.
   _____ d. Mexican beggar boys are cute.
   _____ e. Inflation has reduced the value of the peso.

   Answers and explanations start on page 117.

Read the passage below and answer the questions that follow.

It is 3:30. Do You Know Where Your Child Is?

Many parents do know, and they aren't all that satisfied about it. Take Rose and Curt, for example. They have to pay a retired nurse $100 a week to pick up their six-year-old child from school and care for him until they get home. Helen, a single parent, can barely afford to pay $40 a week to an elderly woman who cares for five other children in her small apartment.

The child-care crisis in America has turned into one of the hottest social issues of the 1980s. But is there really a crisis? Yes, if you are a working parent who cannot afford adequate child care.

Many critics of America's child-care policies have voiced their opinions on this issue. Some support the Swedish model of a government-funded day-care center on every corner. Others like Ed Ziegler, the psychologist who helped launch Project Head Start during the 1970s, feel that the best solution to the child-care crisis lies in the hands of the school system. According to Ziegler, the school should be thought of as a building, not as an institution. He feels that the schools should open earlier in the morning and stay open later in the afternoon. In addition, they should be staffed with child development associates to serve children of working parents.

Ziegler targeted the before-and-after-school child-care concept because he believes that the biggest part of the child-care problem is actually school-aged children. He reports that there may be as many as 5 million children who go home to empty houses after school. These so-called latchkey children make up more than 50 percent of the children needing child care. According to Ziegler, this would be the easiest part of the problem to solve.

Keeping the schools open would not only solve the problem of latchkey children. It might also reduce other social problems related to the improper care of children.

Based on the information in the passage, write *F* if the statement is a fact, *O* if it is an opinion, and *H* if it is a hypothesis.

_____ **1.** The Swedish government funds a day care center on every street.

_____ **2.** The Swedish government cares more about its children than the U.S. government cares about ours.

_____ **3.** If the school systems in America would use their buildings as child-care centers, more parents would attend P.T.A meetings.

_____ **4.** American taxpayers should support adequate child care for all citizens.

_____ **5.** What Ed Ziegler proposes would cost too much money.

Answers and explanations start on page 117.

Read the passage below, and complete the exercise that follows.

Pretty Poison

They are beautiful, sensitive, and thrive when exposed to music. Some say they perform better when you talk to them, although they can't respond to you. While they may be good companions for you, they may not be good for young children. What are these living things that few homes can do without? Houseplants—ornaments that add life and style to your environment.

According to emergency medical experts at New York University Medical Center, many common houseplants should be avoided as decorations in homes with young children. Dr. Lewis R. Goldfrank, one of the experts, reports that between 5 and 10 percent of all poisoning involves eating the leaves and stalks of plants. And 85 percent of these cases, he says, occur in children under six years old.

Popular houseplants such as dieffenbachia (dee-fen-backia) (dumb cane), monstera (Swiss cheese plant), and philodendron (fil-o-din-dron) are poisonous. Dumb cane, for example, is known to paralyze the vocal chords if eaten. Other poisonous plants are the English ivy, asparagus fern, bird of paradise, and the umbrella plant. Yuletide plants such as holly, poinsettia, and mistletoe also may be dangerous if they are eaten. However, the question of whether or not the popular poinsettia is truly poisonous is occasionally debated during Christmastime.

Symptoms of leaf poisoning include skin rashes, nausea, vomiting, and stomach cramps. Blistering and inflamed lips, gums, and tongue also indicate plant poisoning. To prevent houseplant poisoning, parents should keep poisonous leaves away from toddlers. This measure certainly would sharply reduce the number of emergency room patients caused by poisoning.

1. Based on the information in the passage, write *F* if the statement is a fact, *O* if it is an opinion, and *H* if it is a hypothesis.

    _____ **a.** Plants make a home; every home should have them.

    _____ **b.** Dr. Goldfrank is a medical specialist from New York University Medical Center.

    _____ **c.** Talking to your plants every day will result in greater growth than not talking to them.

    _____ **d.** If parents would stop buying toxic plants, the number of poisoning incidents in the average home would drop.

    _____ **e.** If fewer poisonous houseplants were sold, fewer poison victims would be admitted to emergency rooms.

2. Which is the most likely reason some people claim that poinsettias are not poisonous?

    a. People who like poinsettias are afraid they will disappear from the stores during Christmastime.
    b. If the belief that the plants are poisonous persists, people will not buy poinsettias and sales will suffer.
    c. Christmas is not Christmas without poinsettias around.

THINK & WRITE: Besides houseplants, what are some other products that could cause consumers harm but are defended strongly by their producers? List three products and give the reasons why the producers defend them.

Answers and explanations start on page 117.

Author's Bias

Remember the old saying, "There are two sides to every story?" When a person tells only one side of the story, you cannot weigh the facts and decide for yourself who is right or wrong. You know that a balanced argument usually presents both sides of an issue. Writers who state their positions and discuss opposing points of view respect the readers' ability to weigh the facts and reach an individual decision. However, writers sometimes tell only one side of an issue and disregard opposing ideas. When a piece of writing discusses only one side of an issue, we say that it is one-sided and that the writer is *biased*.

A writer's point of view is generally influenced by attitudes, beliefs, and experiences. Below is one parent's opinion on the issue of forced busing to achieve racial balance. Read the paragraph, and write the six charged words on the lines provided. Are the words positively charged or negatively charged?

"I think that busing children to achieve racial balance and to provide academic exposure is a stupid, harebrained idea. Why should *my* seven-year-old be exposed to people coming in and disrupting our fine school? Why can't those being bused stay in their own neighborhoods and attend their own schools? Furthermore, why should our children be forced to give up their computer and science labs to be bused across town? I tell you, it is unfair to put our children through this turmoil just to satisfy some wrongheaded court ruling."

Charged words: _____ _____ _____

_____ _____ _____

Positive or negative? _____

You should have written these charged words: *stupid, harebrained, disrupting, unfair, turmoil,* and *wrongheaded.* The words are *negatively charged* to get across the point that the writer is against forced busing. However, another parent of a child being bused might take the opposite view. She might see the benefits that her child stands to gain. As demonstrated in this case, the position a person takes on an issue depends largely upon whose interests are at stake and upon the experience of that person.

TIP: Often a writer's bias is indicated by the words *I think* or *in my opinion.* At other times, you must look closely for positively charged or negatively charged words that indicate bias.

A critic's job is to review a book, play, musical performance, painting, or other work of art. The critic evaluates a work and weighs its strengths and weaknesses. In their reviews, critics use descriptive words that indicate an opinion. Read the book review below, and answer the questions that follow.

A Review of *Everything Goes* by Holly Hansen

Holly Hansen's first novel *Everything Goes* is aptly titled. Hansen throws anything and everything but the kitchen sink into her plot. The book is an obvious effort to satisfy the tasteless appetite of today's mass paperback reader. There is so much going on in this book that it was impossible for this reader to focus on the main character.

Hansen promises something for everyone, and she delivers: steamy love scenes, violence for violence's sake, rough language, and foreign settings. The problem is that the reader is so caught up in the action that she doesn't care what happens to the main character, and that is fatal for any novel.

The main character, Reva Raines, is described using all of the standard worn-out phrases. She is a gorgeous, ambitious jet setter who climbs her way to the top of the fashion industry. If this sounds like something out of a televison miniseries, you're right. At least with the miniseries, you can turn it off. But if you were foolish enough to spend $5.95 for Hansen's paperback—tough luck.

If *Everything Goes* is a true measure of Hansen's talent, we should weep for the hundreds of trees that went into the publication of the book. We should also pray that she never gets near a word processor again.

1. What is the critic's opinion of *Everything Goes*?

_____

2. What words and phrases indicate this critic's bias?

_____

_____

_____

3. Would you accept this critic's opinion of the book as reliable? Why or why not?

_____

_____

A clever promoter will often focus only on those parts of a review that are favorable to his or her client. The promoter may even change the original meaning of the review by taking words out of context or by focusing only on part of a statement. When words are omitted, ellipses (...) are used. This mark of punctuation means that certain words are missing from the original. Read the publicity release taken from the preceding book review. Notice how certain words are omitted. Think: How has the real meaning of the critic's review been changed?

- *Everything Goes* is aptly titled ...
- There is something for everyone ...
- ... the reader is so caught up in the action ...
- ... like a television miniseries ...
- ... a true measure of Hansen's talent ...

4. What is the purpose of this advertisement?

_____

_____

5. Would a promoter be wrong for publicizing the book in this way?

_____

_____

6. Does this promotional piece accurately reflect the meaning of the critic's review? Why or why not?

_____

_____

THINK & WRITE: Think of other cases in which the true meaning behind a message is distorted by words taken out of context. Describe such a situation.

Answers and explanations start on page 118.

Stereotypes

New Yorkers are unfriendly.
Chicagoans are gangsters.
New Englanders lack humor.
Southern Californians are "laid back."

To what extent are these statements true? Obviously, *some* may be true in a limited way. However, are these statements true for *all* of the people who live in these regions? Of course not. Yet some people choose to label residents of these areas in this way.

When you make broad statements or maintain beliefs about an entire group of people based on extremely limited or no experience, you are using stereotyped thinking.

A *stereotype* is a fixed image that people have in their minds. This picture prevents them from seeing and judging individuals open-mindedly.

Stereotypes involve prejudice. A prejudice is a prejudgment, in which a person makes a judgment on the basis of insufficient or misleading evidence. Relying on stereotypes represents a form of unsound thinking.

Stereotypes are passed on by movies, television, jokes, contacts with other people who believe in them, and even cartoons. Stereotypes can be harmful to the victim to which they are applied as well as to the person who believes in and uses them.

> **T**IP: To decide whether a message is based on stereotyped thinking, ask yourself, "Do I know any person or thing that does *not* fit this image?" If the answer is yes, you can determine that a stereotype is being used.

As you read the following story by Shirley Jackson, consider the stereotyped thinking being shown. Then answer the questions that follow. The statement *After You, My Dear Alphonse* is a playful exchange between two characters in the story. As you read, keep the significance of this statement in mind.

After You, My Dear Alphonse

Mrs. Wilson was just taking the gingerbread out of the oven when she heard Johnny outside talking to someone.

"Johnny," she called, "you're late. Come in and get your lunch."

"Just a minute, Mother," Johnny said. "After you, my dear Alphonse."

"After *you*, my dear Alphonse," another voice said.

Mrs. Wilson opened the door. "Johnny," she said, "you come in this minute and get your lunch. You can play after you've eaten."

Johnny came in after her, slowly. "Mother," he said, "I brought Boyd home for lunch with me."

"Boyd?" Mrs. Wilson thought for a moment. "I don't believe I've met Boyd. Bring him in, dear, since you've invited him. Lunch is ready."

"Boyd!" Johnny yelled. "Hey, Boyd, come on in!"

"I'm coming. Just got to unload this stuff."

"Well, hurry, or my mother'll be sore."

"Johnny, that's not very polite to either your friend or your mother," Mrs. Wilson said. "Come sit down, Boyd."

As she turned to show Boyd where to sit, she saw he was a Negro boy, smaller than Johnny but about the same age. His arms were loaded with kindling wood. "Where'll I put this stuff, Johnny?" he asked.

Mrs. Wilson turned to Johnny. "Johnny," she said, "what did you make Boyd do? What is that wood?"

"Dead Japanese," Johnny said mildly. "We stand them in the ground and run over them with tanks."

"How do you do, Mrs. Wilson?" Boyd said.

"How do you do, Boyd? You shouldn't let Johnny make you carry all that wood. Sit down and eat lunch, both of you."

"Why shouldn't he carry the wood, Mother? It's his wood. We got it at his place."

"Johnny," Mrs. Wilson said, "go on and eat your lunch."

"Sure," Johnny said. He held out the dish of scrambled eggs to Boyd. "After you, my dear Alphonse."

"After *you*, my dear Alphonse," Boyd said.

"After *you*, my dear Alphonse," Johnny said. They began to giggle.

"Are you hungry, Boyd?" Mrs. Wilson asked.

"Yes, Mrs. Wilson."

"Well, don't you let Johnny stop you. He always fusses about eating, so you just see that you get a good lunch. There's plenty of food here for you to have all you want."

"Thank you, Mrs. Wilson."

"Come on, Alphonse," Johnny said. He pushed half the scrambled eggs onto Boyd's plate. Boyd watched while Mrs. Wilson put a dish of stewed tomatoes beside his plate.

"Boyd don't eat tomatoes, do you, Boyd?" Johnny said.

"*Doesn't* eat tomatoes, Johnny. And just because you don't like them, don't say that about Boyd. Boyd will eat *anything*."

"Bet he won't," Johnny said, attacking his scrambled eggs.

"Boyd wants to grow up and be a big strong man so he can work hard," Mrs. Wilson said. "I'll bet Boyd's father eats stewed tomatoes."

"My father eats anything he wants to," Boyd said.

"So does mine," Johnny said. "Sometimes he doesn't eat hardly anything. He's a little guy though. Wouldn't hurt a flea."

"Mine's a little guy, too," Boyd said.

"I'll bet he's strong, though," Mrs. Wilson said. She hesitated. "Does he . . . work?"

"Sure," Johnny said. "Boyd's father works in a factory."

"There, you see?" Mrs. Wilson said. "And he certainly has to be strong to do that—all that lifting and carrying at a factory."

"Boyd's father doesn't have to," Johnny said. "He's a foreman."

Mrs. Wilson felt defeated. "What does your mother do, Boyd?"

"My mother?" Boyd was surprised. "She takes care of us kids."

"Oh. She doesn't work then?"

"Why should she?" Johnny said through a mouthful of eggs. "You don't work."

"You really don't want any

stewed tomatoes, Boyd?"

"No thank you, Mrs. Wilson," Boyd said.

"No thank you, Mrs. Wilson, no thank you, Mrs. Wilson, no thank you, Mrs. Wilson," Johnny said. "Boyd's sister's going to work, though. She's going to be a teacher."

"That's a very fine attitude for her to have, Boyd," Mrs. Wilson restrained an impulse to pat Boyd on the head. "I imagine you're all very proud of her?"

"I guess so," Boyd said.

"What about all your other brothers and sisters? I guess all of you want to make just as much of yourselves as you can."

"There's only me and Jean," Boyd said. "I don't know yet what I want to be when I grow up."

"We're going to be tank drivers, Boyd and me," Johnny said. "Zoom." Mrs. Wilson caught Boyd's glass of milk as Johnny's napkin ring, suddenly transformed into a tank, plowed heavily across the table.

"Look, Johnny," Boyd said. "Here's a foxhole. I'm shooting at you."

Mrs. Wilson, with the speed born of long experience, took the gingerbread off the shelf and placed it carefully between the tank and the foxhole.

"Now eat as much as you want to, Boyd," she said. "I want to see you get filled up."

"Boyd eats a lot, but not as much as I do," Johnny said. "I'm bigger than he is."

"You're not much bigger," Boyd said. "I can beat you running."

Mrs. Wilson took a deep breath. "Boyd," she said. Both boys turned to her. "Boyd, Johnny has some suits that are a little too small for him, and a winter coat. It's not new, of course, but there's lots of wear in it still. And I have a few dresses that your mother or sister could probably use. Your mother can make them over into lots of things for all of you, and I'd be very happy to give them to you. Suppose before you leave I make up a big bundle and then you and Johnny can take it over to your mother right away . . ." Her voice trailed off as she saw Boyd's puzzled expression.

"But I have plenty of clothes, thank you," he said. "And I don't think my mother knows how to sew very well, and anyway I guess we buy just about everything we need. Thank you very much, though."

"We don't have time to carry that old stuff around, Mother," Johnny said. "We got to play tanks with the kids today."

Mrs. Wilson lifted the plate of gingerbread off the table as Boyd was about to take another piece. "There are many little boys like you, Boyd, who would be very grateful for the clothes someone was kind enough to give them."

"Boyd will take them if you want him to, Mother," Johnny said.

"I didn't mean to make you mad, Mrs. Wilson," Boyd said.

"Don't think I'm angry, Boyd. I'm just disappointed in you, that's all. Now let's not say anything more about it."

She began clearing the plates off the table, and Johnny took Boyd's hand and pulled him to the door. "Bye, Mother," Johnny said. Boyd stood for a minute, staring at Mrs. Wilson's back.

"After you, my dear Alphonse," Johnny said, holding the door open.

"Is your mother still mad?" Mrs. Wilson heard Boyd ask in a low voice.

"I don't know," Johnny said. "She's screwy sometimes."

"So's mine," Boyd said. He hesitated. "After *you*, my dear Alphonse."

1. The title of the story *After You, My Dear Alphonse* is appropriate mainly because it

   a. shows the courtesy and respect the boys have for each other
   b. is a secret code phrase used by the boys
   c. is unrelated to the true subject of the story

2. The line *"Dead Japanese," Johnny said mildly. "We stand them in the ground and run over them with tanks"* is a clue that

   a. the two boys are prejudiced against Japanese
   b. the boys are playing war
   c. the story was written around the time of World War II
   d. both *a* and *b*
   e. both *b* and *c*

3. The image of Boyd carrying kindling wood suggests the idea of

   a. strength
   b. slavery
   c. Johnny's laziness

4. Give three direct statements from the story that indicate Mrs. Wilson's stereotyped thinking about blacks.

   a. _____

   b. _____

   c. _____

5. Why does Mrs. Wilson offer Boyd the clothes? What assumption does she make about Boyd's family?

_____

_____

_____

6. Contrast Johnny's behavior toward Boyd with his mother's. How is he different from his mother?

_____

_____

_____

7. Mrs. Wilson's entire conversation is filled with stereotypical undertones. What statements at the end indicate that the boys do not understand Mrs. Wilson's behavior?

_____

_____

_____

THINK & WRITE: In recent years, well-known people in sports have been fired for furthering stereotypes in the media. Los Angeles Dodger manager Al Campanis and CBS sportscaster Jimmy the Greek were fired for making public remarks that were stereotyped and biased. Do you think such firings were justified? Why or why not?

Answers and explanations start on page 118.

What Logic Is Followed?

The logic that a writer uses often depends on his or her purpose for writing. If the writer's purpose is to inform or to explain, the reasoning has to be orderly, accurate, and logical. All the loose ends must be tied. The writer will explain by example, break down complex ideas, and will even use pictures or diagrams to help the reader understand.

On the other hand, if the writer's purpose is to persuade, or to sway the reader's opinion, the writer may not necessarily use logic. He or she may even slant information in such a way as to direct the reader's thinking or behavior along certain lines. You can be on guard against accepting information that may not be sound by being able to recognize the reasoning methods that lie behind a message. In this final chapter, you will practice your skills in understanding two methods of reasoning that writers use. You will learn about

- analogy
- persuasive techniques

Analogy

An analogy is a form of comparison and contrast. It suggests similarities between two things that are otherwise unalike. An analogy can be written as a word analogy in which relationships between certain words are shown, or it can be the framework around which an entire message is written.

In the essay by Sydney J. Harris that you read earlier, an analogy is made between writing and music. We can show this relationship as a word analogy in shorthand:

words : writer :: _____ : composer

This means "Words are to a writer as _____ are to a composer."

To complete this analogy, you need to determine the connection between two words and then find the other pair of words that have a similar relationship. Your thinking should follow this pattern:

QUESTION: What is the relationship of writer to composer?
ANSWER: Writers and composers are types of artists.
INFERENCE: If writers and composers are types of artists, and writers use *words*, then composers must use *notes*.

Let's rewrite the analogy to show the thinking pattern:

used by artists

Words are to a writer as *notes* are to a composer.

types of artists

The analogy is sound. Although writing and composing are different, words are the writer's tools just as notes are the tools of the composer.

The next exercise gives you practice in working with a word analogy. Supply the word that shows the relationship in the analogy. Then complete the steps that follow.

Furnace is to warm as air conditioner is to _____.

Complete the thinking pattern by answering the following question and describing the inference.

QUESTION: What is the relationship between *furnace* and *air conditioner*?

ANSWER: _____

INFERENCE: If a furnace keeps you warm, then an air conditioner

_____

You should have completed the analogy with answers similar to these:

- Furnace is to warm as air conditioner is to cool.
- Both are equipment that *affect a room's temperature.*
- If a furnace keeps you warm, then an air conditioner *keeps you cool.*

This analogy is sound because a furnace produces warm air just as an air conditioner produces cool air.

Now, write your own word analogy using these terms: *brush, sculptor, painter, chisel.* Write the analogy first in sentence form, then in shorthand using the dots that you saw on page 95.

sentence form: _____

shorthand form: _____

You should have written: *brush is to painter as chisel is to sculptor, and brush : painter :: chisel : sculptor*. Another way of writing it would be *chisel is to sculptor as brush is to painter, and chisel : sculptor :: brush : painter*.

In many cases, writers use analogies to show the relationship between an idea that is familiar to the reader and one that is unfamiliar. If you understand one idea, sometimes you can relate it to a new and different idea. Good writers use analogies in literature, science, and social studies materials.

Usually, analogies are sound. However, sometimes writers or speakers use analogies in which the relationships of the ideas being compared are neither clear nor similar. These are faulty analogies.

> **T**IP: To determine if a writer's analogy is sound, decide whether the the ideas being compared resemble each other or have similar properties. If no resemblance or similar properties exist, then the analogy is unsound.

The passage below uses analogy to show the relationship between two different ideas. Read the passage, and answer the questions that follow.

Impeaching a President

Impeaching a president is like [performing] major surgery. It is an act that should not be done hastily or emotionally, and only when it is necessary to restore the well-being of the patient, in this case the government of the nation. The purpose of the surgery is not to punish the diseased organ; neither is the purpose of impeachment to punish a president. In both situations the only legitimate purpose is to remove a source of serious trouble and reestablish a healthy condition.

A surgeon does not initiate the decision to operate. Before he [or she] has been called onto the case, the patient has been examined by a physician who must satisfy himself by the evidence of laboratory tests and x-rays that an operation may be necessary. When the surgeon is consulted, he [or she] reviews the evidence and makes the final decision. A similar procedure is followed in impeachment. The House first studies the question, seeks all pertinent evidence, and then decides whether the matter should go to the Senate. The Senate reviews the evidence and makes the final decision. The whole process of deciding what to do in either surgery or impeachment may take several months.

Both surgery and impeachment are periods of stress for everybody involved. And just as the patient may suffer post-surgical shock, so may the political body suffer from the shock of impeachment. In view of the possible consequences, neither action should be undertaken unless there is no satisfactory alternative. But when the patient's health depends on cutting out the source of the infection, failure to act, in both surgery and impeachment, may have serious consequences.

1. *Impeachment* is to *presidency* as *surgery* is to _____.

    a. illness

    b. patient

    c. organ

2. List five ways in which impeachment and surgery are alike.

    a. _____

    b. _____

    c. _____

    d. _____

    e. _____

3. *Surgeon* is to *operation* as *Senate* is to _____.

    a. government

    b. impeachment

    c. presidency

4. House of Representatives is to the impeachment decision as _____ is to the operating decision.

    a. president

    b. physician

    c. surgeon

5. Is the comparison between impeaching a president and performing major surgery sound? Why or why not?

_____

Read the unsound analogies below, tell what two ideas are being compared, and explain why the analogies are unsound.

6. How can the candidate run the city effectively when he can't even remember to pay his gas bill?

Ideas being compared: _____

The analogy is unsound because _____

_____

7. If the average American family must live within its means, so should the U.S. government. Then we wouldn't be faced with such a huge budget deficit.

Ideas being compared: _____

The analogy is unsound because _____

_____

Answers and explanations start on page 118.

Persuasive Techniques

Persuasion is a part of everyday life. It is a form of communication that convinces people to do, think, feel, or believe what the persuader wants them to. For example, if you have ever been convinced to attend an event because "everybody who is anybody is going to be there," you were persuaded by a technique called *bandwagoning*, which emphasizes joining the crowd.

In addition to bandwagoning, other techniques include *glittering generalities*, testimonial, name-calling, and innuendo. The glittering generality is a type of persuasion in which a speaker uses general and vague terms to influence a person to act. Consider this example:

Brand X is a super gasoline. You may not know it, but your car knows.

Knows is the glittering generality in this case. Just what does your car know, and how does your car know it? The expression is vague. Obviously, this statement is not saying much of anything.

The *testimonial* is a form of persuasion in which a well-known person speaks in favor of or against something. For example, the "Say No to Drugs" campaign started by First Lady Nancy Reagan has gained publicity across the nation primarily because the White House gave it the stamp of approval.

Name-calling is a form of persuasion in which someone attaches an unfavorable name to an idea, person, or group in order to influence the attitude of the audience against the idea or position. The purpose of this type of persuasion is to get the audience to act on emotion rather than logic. Name-calling is shown in the following example:

> Anyone who supports nuclear disarmament for the United States, when Russia is stockpiling nuclear weapons, is a commie pinko conspiring with the enemy.

The terms *commie* (communist) *pinko* (a person who holds radical views) are unfavorable. By classifying all people who support nuclear disarmament as friends of the Soviet Union, the speaker is trying to influence the audience against supporting nuclear disarmament.

Innuendo is a tactic used to persuade a person or group that someone else might have something to hide:

> Why did the town council have a secret meeting so soon after the mayor's death? Do they know something we don't know?

The speaker hints that council members are planning something that should be hidden from the public. But is this necessarily true? Isn't it possible that they wanted to keep an important meeting a secret to discuss urgent town business?

Persuasive techniques are used widely in advertising and in politics. The best way to be on guard against them is to be familiar with the different ways in which the media seek to influence the public.

In the exercise below, read the comments, and determine which form of persuasion is being used. Write the name of the technique on the line provided.

1. "Everyone on your route has ordered a *Times* mailbox. Why should you be left out?" _____

2. "Baby Silk lotion is the most effective product of its kind."

_____

3. "Judge, I don't want this homewrecker to get anywhere near my children because she's a bad influence."

_____

4. "Don't you find it odd that everybody voted against the new stadium except the two councilmen, Calloway and Robertson, who have interests in a construction company?"

_____

5. "If Michael Jackson drinks Pepsi-Cola, it's certainly good enough for me."

_____

For number 1, you should have written *bandwagoning* because the statement suggests joining the crowd. For number 2, you should have written *glittering generalities* since the general statement does not tell you how the lotion is the most effective of its kind. For number 3, you should have written *name-calling* because the use of the word *homewrecker* is an attempt to negatively influence the judge against a person. For number 4, you should have written *innuendo*. By stating that the two councilmen voted for the stadium and by making a point that they both have interests in a construction company, the statement hints that the councilmen might have something to gain. For number 5, you should have written *testimonial* because the statement connects Michael Jackson, a famous singer, to drinking Pepsi-Cola.

The following letters to the editor present two different points of view about public housing projects. Read the two letters, and identify which of the five persuasive techniques is used in each paragraph. The techniques are listed below. Each technique is used only once in each letter.

bandwagoning	glittering generality	testimonial
	name-calling	innuendo

Letter 1

Dear Editor:

The only solution to the problems that plague our city's public housing projects is to do what was done to the Pruitt-Igoe projects in St. Louis in the seventies—blow the high rises to smithereens. In a matter of minutes, these snake pits that breed crime, illness, and poverty will be gone in a puff of smoke.

1. persuasive technique: _____

Any attempt to improve the projects is like putting cosmetics on a corpse to make it look more attractive. Even the well-loved and respected mayor admitted that trying to manage public housing is an impossible job. If he said it's an impossible job, then we should take his word for it.

2. persuasive technique: _____

St. Louis had the guts to admit what everybody else already knows: Public housing is unmanageable. How can a housing agency manage buildings where thousands of people are stacked like rabbits in cages, where many of the residents don't work and refuse to pay rent? Our city should admit its mistake in building them and correct it. All we have to do is follow St. Louis's brilliant example. What are we waiting for?

3. persuasive technique: _____

A survey comparing the cost of repairing the projects to tearing them down was just completed. The study found that demolishing the structures would be far cheaper than trying to repair them. Getting rid of the projects would do wonders in improving the lives of the residents and would even give them a new lease on life.

4. persuasive technique: _____

Finally, it is a matter of record that nine out of ten members of the housing commission are in favor of tearing down the high rises. The only opposing member is Commissioner Greene. Does he really care so much about where the displaced residents will live, or could it be that he is getting something in return for opposing the idea?

5. persuasive technique: _____

Personally, I am so much in favor of this solution that I'd be happy to light the fuse.

Sincerely,

Mr. Joe Blow

Letter 2

Dear Editor:

Dynamiting the high-rise housing projects is not the way to solve our housing problems, no matter what Joe Blow thinks. In fact, it is such a reckless idea that I cannot understand why you wasted precious space on such a letter. Could it be that he is expressing your editorial board's true views?

1. persuasive technique: _____

Our city is *not* St. Louis. This is *not* the 1970s. If the projects are destroyed, where will the homeless residents live? In Joe Blow's neighborhood? I doubt it. People like him were the ones who fought so hard against having low-rise scattered-site housing built in their neighborhoods. We can't even provide housing for the homeless who live on the streets now. What would we do with thousands added to their numbers? Weak-thinking people like Mr. Joe Blow who live in their ivory towers are the main ones who cause the problems we have.

2. persuasive technique: _____

Our projects are an affordable alternative for people who have nowhere else to go. Just because a person comes from the projects does not mean that he or she can't contribute to society. Take Julius Giles, public housing's most famous former resident. He was raised in the projects and owns a multimillion-dollar business today. He's on record as saying he's against tearing the projects down. Why else would he spend his spare time visiting the youngsters, encouraging them to stay in school? If he survived, so can anyone else.

3. persuasive technique: _____

No, the problems in public housing cannot be solved by blowing the buildings up. They can be solved only by giving the residents more involvement in decision making. It's already being done in the low-rise buildings, and it's working in other parts of the city. Let's get with it and get behind this policy for *all* the projects.

4. persuasive technique: _____

Only by giving the residents themselves a chance to manage their property and make decisions that affect their lives can we eliminate the problems Mr. Blow mentions. If given the chance, I'm sure the residents can run the property much better than the current members of the housing board. The residents will be able to provide unlimited opportunities for change and improvement. One thing is for certain. The residents themselves can't do any worse.

Sincerely,

Mrs. Bea Smartt

5. persuasive technique: _____

THINK & WRITE: Advertisements use persuasive techniques all the time. Think of an advertisement that uses one of the techniques above. Which technique does it use? How is that technique effective in selling the product?

Answers and explanations start on page 119.

Skill Review

In this exercise you will have a chance to practice many of the skills you learned in the critical-thinking section of this book.

Educational reform is a major issue that has been receiving widespread attention in recent years. Many people, including educators and politicians, have focused on the need to improve education in the United States. The following editorial addresses one aspect of the educational reform issue: the teaching profession.

Directions: Included in this editorial are examples of invalid conclusions, unsound analogies, author's bias, and persuasive techniques. Read the editorial carefully to apply the critical-thinking skills you've learned in this book.

Editorial

Teachers: An Endangered Species

According to a recent study, the average starting salary for a teacher is nearly $15,000. In contrast, the average beginning engineer earns about $26,000, and the average entry-level job in business administration pays close to $21,000. At such low beginning salaries, is it any wonder that our schools have trouble attracting people to teach? Increasing numbers of teachers leave the field each year, and the school-age population is growing. These facts indicate that the problem will only worsen in coming years.

Another reason why teachers are an endangered species is a lack of respect for them. Teachers' lowly status in our society is summed up in this saying: "Those who *can*, do; those who *can't*, teach." In other words, the real movers and shakers in our society, the people who are making contributions, are *not* teachers. Yet who must educate the movers and shakers? That's right: teachers.

Teachers in Europe, especially in France and Germany, have long been members of an honored profession. Candidates to become teachers must undergo a great deal of training, and the competition for teaching appointments is keen. Other countries pay more than lip service to education. Why can't we? If the United States raises the pay and the level of respect for teaching, more good candidates will be drawn to the field.

Over the past few decades, women have replaced men in the teaching profession. Years ago, when males dominated the teaching profession, they were given respect. As a result, there was not the breakdown in discipline that exists in the schools today. Men took their jobs seriously and devoted the time necessary to do a good job in the classroom. Today, however, with mostly women in the classroom, teachers are viewed as little more than high-priced baby-sitters. It stands to reason that the fields dominated by men receive more respect than those dominated by women. To get more men back into the classrooms, we will have to pay them enough money to support their families.

Teachers are often described today as being incompetent and lazy. Many people think that the qualified teaching professional is the exception. To make matters worse, nonteachers complain that teachers have it easy. After all, teachers put in fewer than eight hours a day, have Christmas and spring breaks, and get the summer off. What these critics fail to consider is that teachers must plan lessons and grade papers on their own time. Summers off are without pay, requiring some teachers to find summer jobs just to make ends meet. As for the breaks, teachers *need* these periods of rest. They need the time to recuperate from the burnout caused by working with children day in and day out. Anyone who thinks teachers have it easy should exchange places with one for a day—for an *hour*.

In the teaching field, there exists something called the self-fulfilling prophecy. Some pupils are told by a teacher that they cannot learn. The teacher's expectations for them are low. They are repeatedly discouraged in their work and given poor grades. Later, these same children, in the care of a supportive teacher, are told that they *are* smart and *can* learn. The teacher's expectations for them are high. After repeated praise, the children begin to live up to the teacher's expectations.

If the self-fulfilling prophecy can work for pupils, it can work for teachers. We must treat teachers as if they are valued and respected, and pay them as much as we pay other people who are respected and valued. Only then will teachers avoid being the Rodney Dangerfields who get no respect.

What can you do? You can lobby your representatives in Congress. You can demand that teachers' salaries be raised. You can get behind the movement for educational reform that is sweeping the country. Our children's lives are at stake.

1. Place a check before the statements from the editorial that are invalid conclusions.

   _____ **a.** Female teachers outnumber male teachers in the schools today.

   _____ **b.** Women teachers are not respected as much as men teachers.

   _____ **c.** Schools lack discipline because fewer men teach today.

   _____ **d.** Fields dominated by men receive more respect than those dominated by women.

   _____ **e.** Teachers are leaving the field because the pay is low.

   _____ **f.** Male teachers take their jobs more seriously than do female teachers.

2. The author of the editorial makes statements that show bias against women. Write at least two statements from the editorial that reflect this view.

   _____

   _____

   _____

3. Based on the information in the editorial, write *F* if the statement is a fact, *O* if it is an opinion, and *H* if it is a hypothesis.

   _____ **a.** The average teacher's starting salary is low compared to the average salary of a beginning engineer.

   _____ **b.** Teachers should be paid as much as other professionals who have an equal amount of education.

   _____ **c.** Teachers have an easy career.

   _____ **d.** If the pay and level of respect for teaching are raised, more good teachers will be drawn to the field.

   _____ **e.** Men will return to the classrooms if they can earn enough to support their families.

4. By comparing the average salaries of a beginning teacher, engineer, and employee in business administration, the writer implies that teaching

   a. is undervalued
   b. is overvalued
   c. has no value

5. Write two statements from the editorial that support the belief that U.S. teachers have low status.

_____

_____

_____

6. What stereotype about teachers is mentioned in this editorial?

_____

_____

_____

7. The writer describes the self-fulfilling prophecy and draws an analogy between pupils whose performance is low and teachers whose status is low. The analogy is unsound because

   a. pupils' performance is *not* related directly to what a teacher expects of them
   b. teachers' performance is *not* related directly to their status in the eyes of the public
   c. teachers' performance can't be measured while pupils' performance can

8. The title "Teachers: An Endangered Species" also suggests an analogy between teachers and endangered species of plants and animals. Endangered species are plants and animals that are threatened by extinction. Name one way in which teachers and endangered species are alike.

_____

_____

9. What two forms of persuasion described earlier in this section are shown in the editorial? Choose from bandwagoning, name-calling, glittering generalities, innuendo, and testimonial.

_____

_____

10. Give one example of each form of persuasion from the editorial.

_____

_____

_____

Answers and explanations start on page 119.

CHAPTER 1: WHAT IS THE MESSAGE?
Stated Main Idea
Rosa Parks Sparks Boycott
pages 4–5

WHO: Rosa Parks
WHAT: sparked the Montgomery bus boycott
WHERE: Montgomery, Alabama
WHEN: December 1, 1955
HOW: by refusing to give up her seat

MAIN IDEA SENTENCE: On December 1, 1955, Rosa Parks sparked the Montgomery bus boycott in Montgomery, Alabama, by refusing to give up her seat.

Tired Hearts
page 6

1. e The facts in the passage state that, after a triathlon, the heart did not contract as well with each beat. However, 24 hours later, the heart worked normally. This points to the main idea that an overworked heart does not work at peak levels.

2. a The reliability of the sports researchers has nothing to do with the way the heart works. All of the other choices are related to the working of the heart.

Poor Girl
pages 7–8

1. c The lines "You've got another love" and "If I try to tell her what I know/She'll misunderstand and make me go" suggest that the speaker wants to give advice to her former boyfriend's new girlfriend but is hesitant to do so.

2. b The words *poor girl* suggest pity. A person who is sympathetic to another, and who wants to advise her, would feel pity, not fear or innocence.

The Unstated Main Idea
Résumé
page 10

1. c The poem describes the effects of different ways of killing yourself. It ends with the statement: "You might as well live." This indicates that the poem is about suicide.

2. c The poet shows that each of the seven ways of committing suicide has negative effects. This suggests that living is a better choice and that suicide is more trouble than it's worth.

3. a The definition of résumé as a short account of a person's qualifications for seeking a job has nothing to do with the poem. The poem concerns going on with one's life. It also is a summary of ways to kill oneself.

4. a Suicide is a serious problem among youth in American society. By treating such a serious subject with humor, the writer is able to communicate effectively the message that life is worth living. The poet uses rhyme, but it is not the main reason for the poem's effectiveness.

Internal Revenue Service cartoon
page 11

1. c The taxpayer's reply to the robber upon leaving the IRS office means that the robber is too late because the IRS had earlier "robbed" the taxpayer.

2. a, d, There are no facts to support the
   f, g statements that the taxpayer has money in his briefcase, that he is being arrested, or that the gunman wants to kill the taxpayer.

Alcohol Passage
pages 12–13

1. d The entire passage discusses the effect of alcohol on different people. Choice *a* is advice that the article doesn't give, and choice *c* is off the topic. Although the passage explains why men can consume more alcohol than women, it is a detail and not the main idea.

2. a, c, e The passage does not support the statement that women do not get drunk as quickly as men. In fact, the opposite is stated.

3. c Of the choices listed, the facts in the passage can explain only why some men try to take advantage of women who drink.

4. Five things from the passage that can determine how quickly a person may get drunk are:
   (1) how fast alcohol is absorbed into the bloodstream
   (2) how quickly it is eliminated from the body
   (3) the amount of water the drinker's body contains
   (4) the percentage of body fat a person has (or size)
   (5) whether the drinker is a male or a female

Inferences

"Experience" cartoon
page 15

1. b The cartoon shows two images: a person looking for a job and a candidate running for the office of president of the United States. The ordinary citizen is turned away because he lacks experience, but the politician does not need any. By putting the two ideas together, the cartoonist is suggesting that a double standard exists.

2. b Of the choices given, only Pat Robertson, a religious leader, had never held a political office when he ran for president.

Left and Right Brain Power
page 16

1. d The only choice that is suggested by the passage is that left-brain and right-brain people approach problems differently.

2. You could have chosen three of the following pieces of evidence to support your inference:
   - The left half controls the ability to see detailed patterns; the right half controls the ability to see the whole picture.
   - Left-brained people tend to be better at performing detail-oriented work; right-brained people tend to be better at performing tasks that require the ability to see the "big picture."
   - Visual responses are different for each half of the brain.
   - The left half of the brain focuses on special facial features; the right half usually sees the entire face.

3. trees, forest
   Trees refers to details; *forest* refers to the larger picture.

4. The expression is generally used as a put-down for detail-oriented people, or left-brain dominant people.

Monkey's Paw
pages 17–18

1. c The monkey's paw brings sorrow and suffering to the three people who ask it to grant wishes. This fact suggests that the best title among the choices is: "Be Careful About What You Ask for—You Just Might Get It."

2. d Mrs. White is grief stricken upon her son's death and wishes him alive again. This is contrary to choice *d*, that she cares more about the insurance money than she does about her son.

3. no The story does not take place in the United States. The clue word that helps to determine this fact is *pounds*. A pound is a unit of money used in Great Britain.

4. Mr. White's second wish is for his son's return to life. The clue that helps determine this is that, after his son dies and Mr. White makes a second wish, he hears a loud knocking at the door.

5. Mr. White's third wish is for Herbert's spirit to rest in peace. The clue that helps determine the answer is that, after Mr. White makes the wish, the knocking stops.

Conclusions from Facts

Pie Graphs—Offenders and Victims
pages 20-21

1. **a.** 18%
   b. 56% (38% + 18%)
   c. 18%
   d. 21% (17% + 4%)

2. **a. no** The graph does not concern the number of robberies reported.

   b. yes By adding the percentage of murders committed by acquaintances of the victims (38%) to the percentage of murders committed by relatives (18%), you arrive at a total of 56%. This means that most victims of homicides know the people who kill them.

   c. yes The percentages of people killed by strangers and relatives both are 18%.

   d. no The graph does not compare the number of robberies to the number of violent crimes committed.

   e. yes The graph shows that 75% of robberies are committed by strangers—the greatest percentage of all categories shown.

   f. yes The percentage of robberies committed by strangers (75%) is greater than the percentage of murders committed by strangers (18%).

Manchild in the Promised Land
pages 21-22

1. According to the passage, the mother is willing to withstand the cold and to buy spoiled meat rather than complain. Both of these facts support the statement that she is willing to risk her health.

2. The son pawns his ring so that he and his mother can take a cab to the housing office. This indicates unselfishness.

3. The passage mentions cold weather and a snowstorm.

4. The references to 145th Street and Broadway, two streets mainly identified with New York City.

Zits Can Give Teens Fits
page 23

1. **yes** The passage describes the various stages of acne.

2. **no** The passage cautions people to avoid fatty and acidic foods but does not state that fats and acids are the chief causes of acne.

3. **yes** The first sentence of the passage states that acne is a common skin problem for teenagers.

4. **no** Dirty skin is not mentioned as a cause of acne.

5. **yes** Fatty acids contain oils, so they increase the amount of oil in the body.

6. **yes** The passage states that acne is especially common during the teen years because the production of sex hormones increases.

Predictions and Outcomes

One Flew over the Cuckoo's Nest
pages 25-26

1. **d** The statements "We do not impose certain rules and restrictions on you without a great deal of thought" and "What can we do? You can't be arrested. You can't be put on bread and water. . . . What can we do?" both add up to the prediction that the men will have one of their favorite privileges taken away.

2. **c** The passage makes no mention of the men's lack of job skills in the outside world.

The Insurance Game
pages 27-29

1. **c** The passage states, "The company is gambling that most young people will live through the year." A gamble is a bet based on evaluating certain odds. A dice game and a lottery operate differently than a bet.

2. **c** The amount of insurance premiums are determined by how long people in a given population are expected to live. If women's premiums are lower than men's, then you can conclude that women generally live longer than men. It is a faulty generalization that women are healthier than men.

3. **b** Of the three choices, only health has a direct relationship to the length of a person's life.

4. a. 71.9 years
   b. 77.3 years
   c. 4.3 years less
   d. 4.2 years longer

5. a. F At every age level of the chart, women's life expectancy is higher than men's.

   b. T Women who were 65 years old in 1980 were expected to live 17.3 more years; men of the same age were expected to live 14 more years.

   c. F At the ages of 10, 15, and 20, both males and females had many years left to live.

   d. F Men who were 30 years old in 1980 could be expected to live until the age of 73.2.

CHAPTER 2: WHAT PATTERN IS FOLLOWED?

Cause and Effect

Plaque Attack
pages 32-33

1. The order may vary:
   a. eating on the run
   b. not flossing
   c. not brushing

2. Gingivitis is the first stage of gum disease that untreated plaque leads to.

3. Periodontitis is the advanced stage of gum disease that untreated plaque leads to.

4. Tooth loss is the final result of untreated gum disease.

5. Plaque-fighting toothpastes have resulted from dentists' warnings about the dangers of plaque.

Cop-outs for Dropouts
pages 34-36

1. In some urban communities, almost half of the ninth graders drop out before they complete high school.

2. d lack of dedicated teachers
   e inadequate teaching of basic skills

3. a lack of support from parents
   c school administrators

4. a too little government funding
   c unprepared and undedicated teachers

5. b peer group pressure
   c lack of parental support
   d overcrowded classes

Against the Odds
pages 36-37

1. Answers will vary. Possible causes of Terry's fall are a twisted ankle and overeagerness to win the game.

2. The effects of Terry's fall were (1) a fractured kneecap requiring extensive knee surgery and (2) postponement of a possible pro basketball career.

3. b According to the passage, an athlete who suffered an injury similar to Terry's was back on the court within a year.

4. a The statement "down, but not down for the count" suggests that Terry is not giving up on his career goal.

5. Answers will vary. "Against the Odds" is an appropriate title because it shows an athlete's determination to "beat the odds" and realize his dream.

Sequence

Senior Fights Back
pages 39-40

1. a. 2   **e.** 6
   b. 1   **f.** 5
   c. 3   **g.** 7
   d. 4   **h.** 8

2. b The best statement of the message that underlies the passage is "Looks Are Deceiving" because one would not ordinarily expect a female senior citizen to be able to defend herself.

3. c Sally's ability to defend herself suggests that she had training in self-defense.

4. b The only reasonable prediction based on the events is that the boy will be booked for attempted armed robbery since the witnesses to the crime called the police.

Illustration—Human Reproduction
page 41

Human reproduction is a many-staged process. The father contributes the sperm. The mother contributes the ovum. The parents' sex cells unite into a fertilized ovum. The fertilized ovum divides into two cells. The two cells divide into four cells. From four cells, the fertilized ovum divides into eight. Within one month a human embryo is formed. After nine months, the baby is fully formed, a creature that is made up of millions of cells!

Drug Use and Abuse Are Not New
pages 42–44

a. 1800s	**f.** 1832
b. 1980s	**g.** 1900s
c. 1805	**h.** 2700 B.C.
d. 1960s	**i.** 1500 B.C.
e. 1893	**j.** 1700s

2. a. T The passage discusses the medical uses of certain drugs.

   b. T The passage mentions the addictive powers of opium and cocaine.

   c. F The passage mentions marijuana's effectiveness in counteracting the nauseous side effects of chemotherapy.

   d. T All of the drugs described in the passage come from plants.

   e. T The passage mentions England's use of heroin as a painkiller and states that it is illegal in the United States.

Comparison and Contrast
Worlds Apart
pages 46–48

1. a. Both are 25 years old.
   b. Both live in South Africa.
   c. Both work at the same mine.

2. Exact wording may vary. You could have listed five of these six differences:
   a. Simon can't vote in national elections; Pieter can.
   b. Simon is black; Pieter is white.
   c. Simon lives in poverty; Pieter does not.
   d. Simon is a laborer; Pieter is a foreman.
   e. Simon earns $200 a month; Pieter earns $200 a week.
   f. Simon is likely to be less educated than Pieter.

3. The answers below show from highest to lowest:

Percent of population:
blacks, whites, coloreds, Asians

Literacy level:
whites, Asians, coloreds, blacks

Money spent on education:
whites, Asians, coloreds, blacks

4. a. however
   b. although
   c. different
   d. contrasted to
   e. while

Smoking, Thumb Sucking, and . . . Lollipops
pages 49–50

1. a. are bad habits
   b. have bad effects on the victim's health
   c. are described as being relaxing
   d. satisfy the need for oral stimulation

2. a. T	**e. T**
b. S	**f. T**
c. S	**g. S**
d. S	

3. Effects of smoking cited in the passage are lung cancer, heart disease, and other respiratory diseases.

4. Effects of thumb sucking cited in the passage are crooked teeth and lisping.

5. You may have chosen five of these "contrast" words contained in the passage: but, though, while, nevertheless, differences, on the other hand, and however.

6. a. in common
   b. both
   c. similarity

7. a. to begin
   b. second
   c. third
   d. finally

Friends' Advice
pages 51–53

1. out of sight, out of mind
2. no news is good news
3. you're never too old to learn
4. a bird in the hand is worth two in the bush
5. he who hesitates is lost
6. still waters run deep
7. d In the story, for every positive statement given, a negative one applies. This suggests that, for most platitudes, it's easy to find an opposite.
8. a. what you don't know can't hurt you
         no news is good news
    b. you can't judge a book by its cover
         still waters run deep
9. Based on the advice given, it would seem that Jan is the true friend because the advice she gives Connie is more encouraging than June's.

CHAPTER 3: WHAT WORDS ARE USED?

Denotation and Connotation

A Writer Needs an Ear for Words
pages 56-57

1. **a.** ate
   b. devoured
   c. glowing
   d. glittered
   e. obesity
   f. plump
   g. unutterable
   h. unspeakable

2. **b** The entire point of the essay concerns the proper use of words. Choices *a* and *c* are details that support the main idea. Choice *d* is not stated.

What's in a Name?
pages 58-59

1. **a.** hair designer or hairstylist
   b. maintenance engineer
   c. sanitation engineer
   d. funeral director or mortician
   e. domestic engineer

2. **c** The passage raises the question of whether or not changes in job titles reflect status consciousness more than the desire for more accurate descriptions. This would seem to imply that, for status conscious people, changes in job titles are more important than for people who are secure in themselves. Choice *a* is stated directly in the passage, and choices *b* and *c* are neither stated nor implied.

SKILL REVIEW

The War Prayer
pages 60-64

1. **c** By pointing out the negative consequences of war, Twain is suggesting that war is a mixed blessing. The other titles do not fit the poem.

2. **a.** 3   **e.** 4
   b. 2   **f.** 7
   c. 1   **g.** 6
   d. 5

3. Exact wording may vary.
   The young men in uniform are held in high esteem because they are going off to war to defend their county.

4. The mood of the church before the stranger's speech is jubilant, joyful. The mood during the speech is hushed.

5. Exact wording may vary.
   Few individuals spoke openly against the war because they were afraid of being viewed as being unpatriotic.

6. In his prayer, the pastor is asking for victory over and protection from the enemy in war. Twain's message is that the request does not seem to befit the role of a pastor because engaging in war goes against the principles of most religions.

7. **a** The stranger pointed out to the congregation the consequences of victory in war. By showing the ill effects of war, he is implying that a just God does not approve of war under any circumstances.

8. You can probably conclude that Twain withheld the poem from publication because of the controversy it would raise by being antiwar in a prowar period.

9. From the man's act of questioning the messenger's sanity, you can infer that people who do not conform to the larger society's ways of thinking are considered to be abnormal.

10. Answers will vary, but it is true that speaking out against war is not as unpopular in recent years as it was in Mark Twain's time.

CHAPTER 4: HOW SOUND IS THE REASONING?

Invalid Conclusions

A Heart Gives Out
pages 67-69

1. **d** The passage cites several health problems that Mayor Washington had that put him in the high risk category. However, the conclusion of the passage suggests that his death was related directly to the political fighting in City Hall. This represents an invalid conclusion based on faulty reasoning.

2. a. I The passage discusses the risk factors involved in heart attacks. Just because a person has high blood pressure, high cholesterol levels, and does not get regular checkups doesn't mean he or she will have a heart attack.

b. V The passage points out that high blood pressure alone doubles the risk of heart attacks, and that blacks develop high blood pressure twice as often as whites and they die from it three times as often.

c. V If obesity, high cholesterol levels, and smoking increase one's risk of suffering a heart attack, then reducing these risk factors would reduce a person's risk.

d. I The passage points out that the mayor's poor physical health was the key factor that contributed to his death, not his love for the city.

e. I People *can* reduce their risk of suffering heart attacks.

3. b The passage says, "Mayor Washington was such a case, despite the state-of-the-art medical care used to revive him." In the way it is used, state-of-the-art means modern.

Twelve Angry Men
pages 70–71

1. a While it may be true that some teenagers from disadvantaged areas are physically abused daily, it is not valid that *all* of them suffer the same fate.

2. d There are exceptions to the rule that teenagers from disadvantaged areas are physically abused daily.

3. Juror Eight appears to show the most concern by his statement that "It's not easy for me to raise my hand and send a boy off to die without talking about it first."

4. Juror Ten appears to show the least concern by his statement that "We don't owe him a thing. He got a fair trial."

Bar Graph—"Married Women Double in the Work Force"
pages 72–73

1. V The percentage of married women who had jobs in 1957 was 33%; the percentage in 1987 was 68%.

2. I The graph does not explain why more married women are working today.

3. V The percentage of single women in the work force for 1957 and 1987 is 80%.

4. I The graph does not deal with reasons why more divorced women are working today.

5. V The percentage of married women working in 1987 was 68%; the percentage of divorced and widowed women who were working was 79%, a difference of 11%.

6. V The graph shows that the majority of married women are working today (68%) as opposed to only 33% thirty years ago. Assuming that the husbands of these women also have jobs, this fact supports the conclusion that the United States has become primarily a two-income-family nation within the past 30 years.

Values
The Gentleman of Rio en Medio
pages 74–77

1. c Don Anselmo had agreed to sell his land to the Americans for less than it was worth, but was not willing to sell the trees that stood for his family members. These facts support the statement that Don Anselmo was a man of his word who valued family more than money.

2. Answers will vary. Two sentences that show Don Anselmo to be a mannerly and dignified man are: "The old man bowed to all of us," and, "Then he shook hands all around."

3. The Americans demonstrate their respect for the generosity of Don Anselmo by buying the trees from his descendants.

4. The Americans could have put up a *No Trespassing* sign on the property and had the trespassers arrested for overrunning the property.

5. a In the United States, the seller of property seeks the highest price a buyer will pay for property.

6. c The story is titled "Gentleman of Rio en Medio" because the main character acts like a gentleman throughout. He shows the qualities of politeness and loyalty, and he is considerate and respected.

7. b Of the three groups shown, only Native Americans do not perceive land in terms of its dollar value.

Is the "Right to Die" a Wrong Idea?
pages 77–78

1. b The Dutch culture is different than the culture of the United States. The fact that the Dutch are not kept on life-support systems as often as in the United States indicates a value being decided by the needs of the culture.

2. a In the passage, the critics question giving doctors the right to "play God." This argument is based on standards of right and wrong as determined by religion.

Pie Graph—Should Mercy Killing Be Legal?
page 79

1. b Whether the lawyers represent a geographic cross-section of the United States has much to do with the reliability of the information in the graph.

2. a If the percentage of those responding "Don't Know" is added to the percentage responding "Should Not" (11.5 and 31.7 percent) the total would be 43.2 percent. This figure is smaller than the one for those who favor mercy killing (56.8 percent).

3. c Of all the specialties in law listed, the real estate lawyer's opinion would carry the least weight. A specialist in that field would deal less frequently with related issues than would criminal and civil lawyers. Criminal lawyers deal with cases that include physical injury and death. Civil lawyers consider issues that have to do with lawsuits that sometimes involve bodily injury.

Fact, Opinion, and Hypothesis

Curious Tourist, Yankee Gringo
pages 81–82

1. a Of the choices, only a—that if their parents had jobs, many Mexican children would not have to beg American tourists for money—is a hypothesis. You could check this hypothesis by seeing if most of the parents of begging children had jobs.

2. a. O Whether Mexican or Puerto Rican food is tastier is based on a person's feelings.

b. F The passage states that Julia and Miguel are celebrating their first wedding anniversary.

c. F The passage states that Sarah and Sid sit across from Julia and Miguel, who have seats in the tourist section.

d. O Cuteness is a matter of personal opinion.

e. F Data can prove whether inflation has lowered the value of the peso.

It Is 3:30. Do You Know Where Your Child Is?
pages 82–83

1. F This is stated in the article.

2. O It cannot be proved whether the Swedish government or the U.S. government cares more for its children. The level of caring cannot be measured.

3. H The statement could be proved by measuring attendance at PTA meetings after the establishment of child-care centers in schools.

4. O That American taxpayers should support adequate child care is an opinion.

5. O Whether Ziegler's idea about solving the child-care crisis costs too much money depends on one's personal feeling about how much money is "too much."

Pretty Poison
pages 84–85

1. a. O Whether all homes should have plants is a matter of personal taste. The word *should* indicates an opinion.

b. F The passage identifies Goldfrank as a medical expert at New York University Medical Center. This could be verified through the medical center's personnel department.

c. H The results of talking to plants every day can be tested.

d. H The statement that poisoning incidents in the home would drop if parents stopped buying toxic plants can be tested.

e. H The possible relationship between the number of poisonous houseplants sold and the number of poison victims admitted to emergency rooms can be tested.

2. b The best reason given as to why poinsettias would be defended against claims that they are poisonous is that people might not buy them, and as a result, sales would suffer. People who buy poinsettias are not as likely to start a campaign in favor of the plants as people who sell them. The statement that Christmas is not Christmas without poinsettias is a personal opinion.

Author's Bias
A Review of *Everything Goes* by Holly Hansen
pages 87–88

1. The critic thinks *Everything Goes* is a poor novel.

2. Answers will vary. Some words that show the critic's bias against the book are: ". . . an effort to satisfy the tasteless appetite of today's mass paperback reader"; "it was impossible for this reader to focus on the main character"; "the main character is described using all of the standard worn-out phrases"; and "we should weep for the hundreds of trees that went into the publication of this book. We should pray that she never gets near a word processor again."

3. Answers will vary. However, generally critics are well-read people and are knowledgeable about the kinds of books they review.

4. The purpose of the advertisement is to get the public to buy the book in spite of its flaws.

5. Answers will vary. A promoter would be doing his job by publicizing the book in the way described. The words are actually included in the critic's review, but they are taken out of context and distort the critic's intent in favor of the writer.

6. The promotional piece distorts the true meaning of the critic's review by taking out words that are necessary to communicate the reviewer's true feelings.

Stereotypes
After You, My Dear Alphonse
pages 90–94

1. a The title "After You, My Dear Alphonse" shows the courtesy and respect the boys have for each other.

2. e The line *"Dead Japanese . . ."* serves to place the story in time. During World War II, the United States was at war with Japan. Also, the line indicates that the boys are playing war. Throughout the story the boys are never shown as having prejudiced feelings (choice a).

3. b The image of Boyd carrying kindling wood suggests the idea of slavery.

4. Answers may vary. Some statements that indicate Mrs. Wilson's attitude toward blacks are: "Boyd will eat *anything*"; "Boyd wants to grow up and be a big strong man so he can work hard"; "And he certainly has to be strong to do that— all that lifting and carrying at a factory"; and "I guess all of you want to make just as much of yourselves as you can."

5. Mrs. Wilson offers Boyd the clothes because she assumes that Boyd's family is poor.

6. Johnny behaves differently from his mother in that he accepts Boyd for who he is. Unlike Mrs. Wilson, Johnny has no preset ideas about what Boyd or his family should be like.

7. The statements indicating that the boys do not understand Mrs. Wilson's behavior are: " 'She's screwy sometimes.' 'So's mine,' Boyd said."

CHAPTER 5: WHAT LOGIC IS FOLLOWED?
Analogy
Impeaching a President
pages 97–99

1. b The passage shows the similarity between impeaching a president and performing surgery on a sick patient.

2. Impeachment and surgery are alike in that:

a. Both are actions that should not be done hastily or emotionally.

b. Both are procedures whose purpose is to remove a source of serious trouble and reestablish a healthy condition.

c. Both situations require consultation, and a decision may take several months.

d. Both involve periods of stress for everybody concerned.

e. Neither should be undertaken unless there is no alternative.

3. b A surgeon performs the operation on a sick patient; the Senate makes the final decision on impeachment.

4. b Both the House of Representatives and a physician make a preliminary decision, not the final judgment.

5. The comparison made between impeaching a president and performing major surgery is sound because the two procedures, though different, are related to each other in a similar way.

6. The ideas being compared are running a city and paying one's gas bill. The analogy is unsound because running a city requires skills that greatly differ from those needed to manage one's personal finances.

7. The ideas being compared are the American family and the U.S. government. The analogy is unsound because a family's economic needs and resources are different from those of a government involving hundreds of millions of people.

Persuasive Techniques

Letter to the Editor 1
pages 101–103

1. The persuasive technique used is *name-calling*, the tactic of attaching an unfavorable name to an idea. The writer describes the high-rise projects as snake pits.

2. The technique used is *testimonial*, the strategy of identifying a well-known person with a cause. The writer states that the well-loved and respected mayor believed that managing public housing is impossible.

3. The technique used is *bandwagoning*, the tactic of persuading someone to do something just because someone else does it. The writer tries to persuade the city's housing committee to dynamite the projects because St. Louis did it.

4. The technique used is *glittering generalities*, using general and vague terms to influence a person to act. The writer does not say just how getting rid of the buildings will "do wonders" or how it will give the residents a "new lease on life."

5. The technique used is *innuendo*. The paragraph hints that Commissioner Greene may have something to hide, since he is the only member who is against tearing down the projects.

Letter to the Editor 2
pages 103–104

1. The technique used is *innuendo*. The writer is hinting that the newspaper to which she is writing is in favor of dynamiting the projects.

2. The technique used is *name-calling*. The writer describes Joe Blow as "weak-thinking" and accuses him of living in an "ivory tower."

3. The technique used is *testimonial*. The writer mentions a famous former resident who opposes tearing down the high-rise projects.

4. The technique used in the paragraph is *bandwagoning*. The writer suggests that others join in the movement toward resident involvement in decison making.

5. The technique used is *glittering generalities*. The writer does not state what "unlimited opportunities" for change and improvement will follow from residents having a voice in decision making.

SKILL REVIEW

Teachers: An Endangered Species
pages 105–109

1. b The passage says that when males dominated the teaching profession, teachers were given more respect. The decline in respect for teachers could have other causes than the increase in women teachers. Other changes may also have taken place.

c The editorial implies that the increase of female teachers in the schools brought about a breakdown in discipline. This conclusion is invalid because there could be many other causes for the breakdown in discipline in the schools.

d The editorial does not provide evidence to support the statement that fields dominated by men receive more respect than those dominated by women. The passage does not say how much respect people in other fields get.

f The statement that male teachers take their jobs more seriously than female teachers do cannot be supported because seriousness and dedication are not restricted to one sex. Female teachers take their jobs just as seriously as male teachers.

2. Three statements that show bias against women include "Men took their jobs seriously and devoted the time necessary to do a good job in the classroom," implying that women do not; "Today, however, with mostly women in the classroom, teachers are viewed as little more than high-priced baby-sitters;" and "It stands to reason that the fields dominated by men receive more respect than those dominated by women."

3. **a. F** By citing salary figures, the editorial shows that the average beginning salary of a teacher is low compared to the starting salaries of an engineer.

b. O The belief that teachers should be paid as much as other professionals who have an equal amount of education is an opinion. The word *should* indicates an opinion.

c. O It is an opinion that teachers have an easy career. Whether a career is easy depends on a person's standards for judging.

d. H Research could test whether greater pay and respect would lead to an increase in the number of good teachers drawn to the field.

e. H Research could test the relationship between an increase in pay and the number of men (with families) returning to the teaching field. Research could also test whether most men who have given up teaching have families to support.

4. **a** By comparing average salaries for beginners in three fields and showing that teachers earn the least money, the writer implies that teaching is undervalued.

5. Answers will vary. One statement that supports the belief that U.S. teachers have low status is the saying "Those who *can*, do; those who *can't*, teach," which implies that teachers have little ability. Another statement is that teachers are often described as incompetent and lazy. Also, by contrasting the status of teachers in Europe with the status of teachers in the United States, the writer supports the belief that American teachers have relatively low status.

6. A stereotype about teachers mentioned in the essay is that teachers are incompetent and lazy.

7. **b** The analogy is unsound because students' performance *is* related to their teacher's expectations as demonstrated by the editorial's example. Students who have been expected to receive poor grades are given them. The same students who have been expected to perform well do so. On the other hand, teachers' performance is *not* related to their low status in the eyes of the public. To argue that because teachers have low status they perform poorly is unsound reasoning.

8. Answers will vary. Students can choose one of these three ways in which teachers and endangered species are alike:

    (1) The numbers for both are shrinking.

    (2) Teachers and endangered species are valuable resources.

    (3) Both require special action to increase their numbers.

9. Two forms of persuasion shown in the editorial are name-calling and bandwagoning.

10. Examples of name-calling include *high-priced baby-sitters* and the description of teachers as incompetent and lazy. Examples of bandwagoning include the statements *Other countries pay more than lip service to education. Why can't we?* and *You can get behind the movement for educational reform that is sweeping the country.*